The CBT
Art Workbook for
Managing Anger

Part of the CBT Art Workbooks for Mental and Emotional Wellbeing series

The CBT Art Workbooks for Mental and Emotional Wellbeing series provides creative CBT information and worksheets for adults to manage and understand a variety of emotional issues. Suitable for adults in individual or group therapeutic work, they are an excellent resource to use in conjunction with professional therapy or for adults to use themselves to improve and maintain mental wellbeing.

Also part of the CBT Art Workbooks for Mental and Emotional Wellbeing series

The CBT Art Workbook for Managing Stress
Jennifer Guest
ISBN 978 1 78775 098 2
eISBN 978 1 78775 099 9

The CBT Art Workbook for Coping with Depression
Jennifer Guest
ISBN 978 1 78775 096 8
eISBN 978 1 78775 097 5

The CBT Art Workbook for Coping with Anxiety
Jennifer Guest
ISBN 978 1 78775 012 8
eISBN 978 1 78775 013 5

By the same author

The CBT Art Activity Book
100 illustrated Handouts for Creative Therapeutic Work
Jennifer Guest
ISBN 978 1 84905 665 6
eISBN 978 1 78450 168 6

The Art Activity Book for Psychotherapeutic Work
100 Illustrated CBT and Psychodynamic Handouts for Creative Therapeutic Work
Jennifer Guest
ISBN 978 1 78592 301 2
eISBN 978 1 78450 607 0

The Art Activity Book for Relational Work
100 illustrated therapeutic worksheets to use with individuals, couples and families
Jennifer Guest
ISBN 978 1 78592 160 5
eISBN 978 1 78450 428 1

The CBT Art Workbook for Managing Anger

Part of the CBT Art Workbooks for Mental and Emotional Wellbeing *series*

Jennifer Guest

Jessica Kingsley Publishers
London and Philadelphia

First published in 2020
by Jessica Kingsley Publishers
73 Collier Street
London N1 9BE, UK
and
400 Market Street, Suite 400
Philadelphia, PA 19106, USA

www.jkp.com

Copyright © Jennifer Guest 2020

Library of Congress Cataloging in Publication Data
A CIP catalog record for this book is available from the Library of Congress

British Library Cataloguing in Publication Data
A CIP catalogue record for this book is available from the British Library

ISBN 978 1 78775 100 2
eISBN 978 1 78775 101 9

Printed and bound in the United States

Acknowledgements

I would like to express many thanks to all my clients and colleagues, who, over the years, have helped bring this workbook into being. Grateful appreciation goes to the theorists who have devoted their lives and careers to helping people experience happier, healthier and more peaceful lives. I've given credit to theorists where I've knowingly designed a worksheet from their work, and there are some pages designed from techniques I've come across over the years which I'm unfortunately unable to give specific credit to. No worksheets have been created where the source of the credit is known and not mentioned. Thanks also to everyone involved at Jessica Kingsley Publishers for their support and input.

Contents

About This Book

For those experiencing significant levels of anger, this workbook offers an opportunity to help gain some understanding about how to manage and reduce anger levels, using tools from cognitive behavioural therapy (CBT) approaches. I've worked with many clients experiencing anger over the years, and have found CBT ideas have been incredibly successful in helping to lower levels of anger being experienced.

It's a privilege to be able to share these ideas with you here, and I sincerely hope this workbook has a positive impact on your life and your wellbeing.

This book can be used autonomously or in conjunction with therapy. It's not intended to be used as a replacement for cognitive behavioural therapy, if therapeutic input would be beneficial. Please ensure that access to professional support is available if you experience any unexpected or overwhelming emotional reactions as a result of working through this book. Likewise, if the levels of anger you're experiencing are seriously impacting on your ability to function doing your usual daily tasks or carrying out commitments, or are a threat to the safety of yourself or others, please do seek professional help.

You might choose to focus on the pages most relevant to you, or work through the entire book from beginning to end.

Introduction

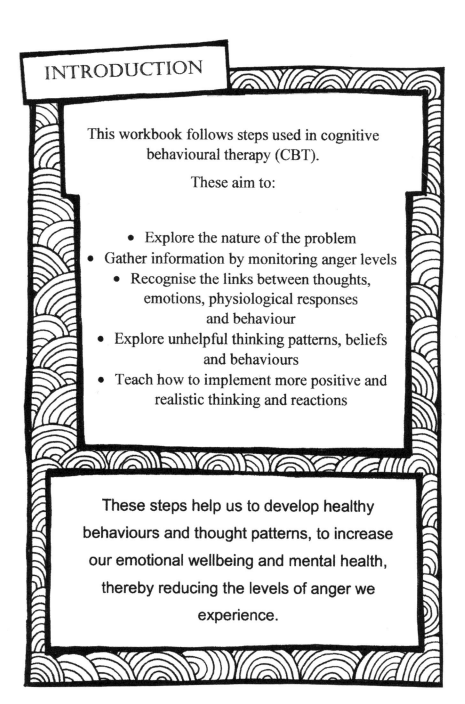

INTRODUCTION

This workbook follows steps used in cognitive behavioural therapy (CBT).

These aim to:

- Explore the nature of the problem
- Gather information by monitoring anger levels
- Recognise the links between thoughts, emotions, physiological responses and behaviour
- Explore unhelpful thinking patterns, beliefs and behaviours
- Teach how to implement more positive and realistic thinking and reactions

These steps help us to develop healthy behaviours and thought patterns, to increase our emotional wellbeing and mental health, thereby reducing the levels of anger we experience.

WHY ART?

Having worked within the therapeutic world for nearly two decades, I consider delivering therapy as one of my passions, alongside art.

Making art has been personally therapeutic during times when I've experienced emotional challenges in my life.

I've witnessed the benefits of art-making and using visual ways of expression and processing with many clients. At the very least, this is a way to encourage relaxation, and, on a more profound level, it can facilitate deeper change. The ideas in this workbook provide a focus for coping with and reducing harmful anger levels through the use of creativity.

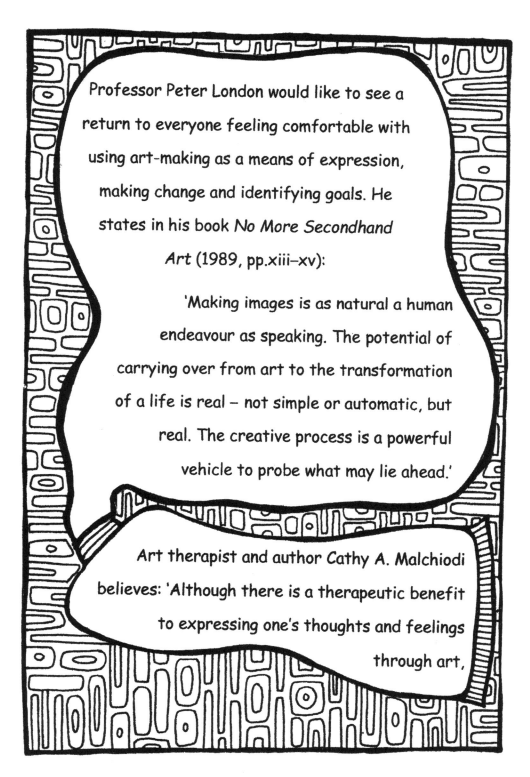

Professor Peter London would like to see a return to everyone feeling comfortable with using art-making as a means of expression, making change and identifying goals. He states in his book *No More Secondhand Art* (1989, pp.xiii–xv):

'Making images is as natural a human endeavour as speaking. The potential of carrying over from art to the transformation of a life is real – not simple or automatic, but real. The creative process is a powerful vehicle to probe what may lie ahead.'

Art therapist and author Cathy A. Malchiodi believes: 'Although there is a therapeutic benefit to expressing one's thoughts and feelings through art,

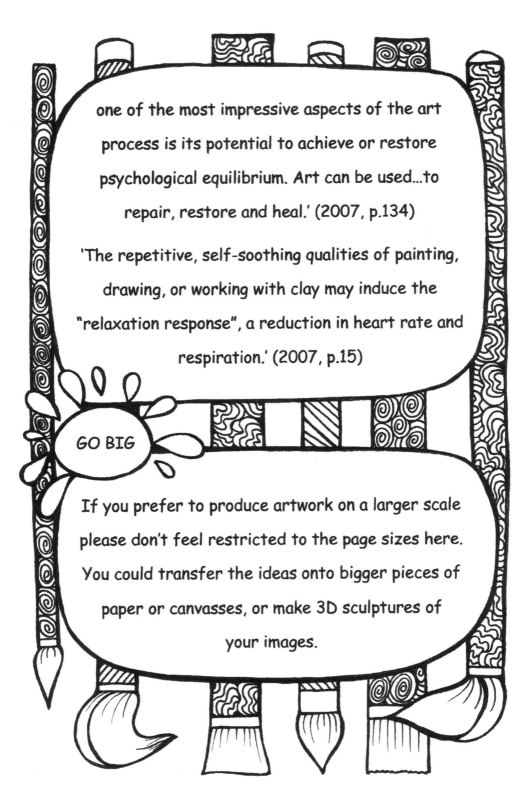

one of the most impressive aspects of the art process is its potential to achieve or restore psychological equilibrium. Art can be used...to repair, restore and heal.' (2007, p.134)

'The repetitive, self-soothing qualities of painting, drawing, or working with clay may induce the "relaxation response", a reduction in heart rate and respiration.' (2007, p.15)

GO BIG

If you prefer to produce artwork on a larger scale please don't feel restricted to the page sizes here. You could transfer the ideas onto bigger pieces of paper or canvasses, or make 3D sculptures of your images.

1

What Is Anger?

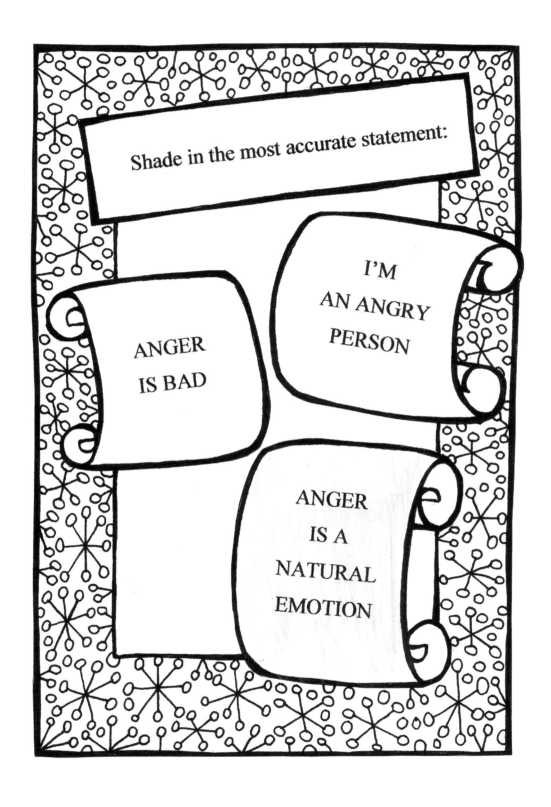

Shade in the most accurate statement:

ANGER IS BAD

I'M AN ANGRY PERSON

ANGER IS A NATURAL EMOTION

WHAT IS **ANGER?**

Anger is an emotion we
all experience.

If you experience anger as:

- Being too intense
- Lasting for too long
- Being too frequent
- Disproportionate to the situation
- Leading to aggression or violence

...then maybe anger has become
problematic.

If you want to **reduce** the anger you're
experiencing, and **manage it effectively**,
then this workbook is for you!

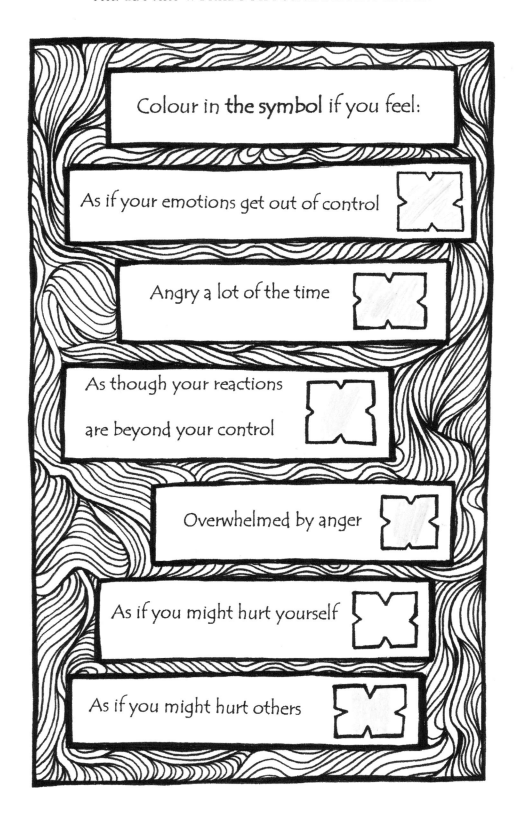

Colour in **the symbol** if you feel:

As if your emotions get out of control

Angry a lot of the time

As though your reactions are beyond your control

Overwhelmed by anger

As if you might hurt yourself

As if you might hurt others

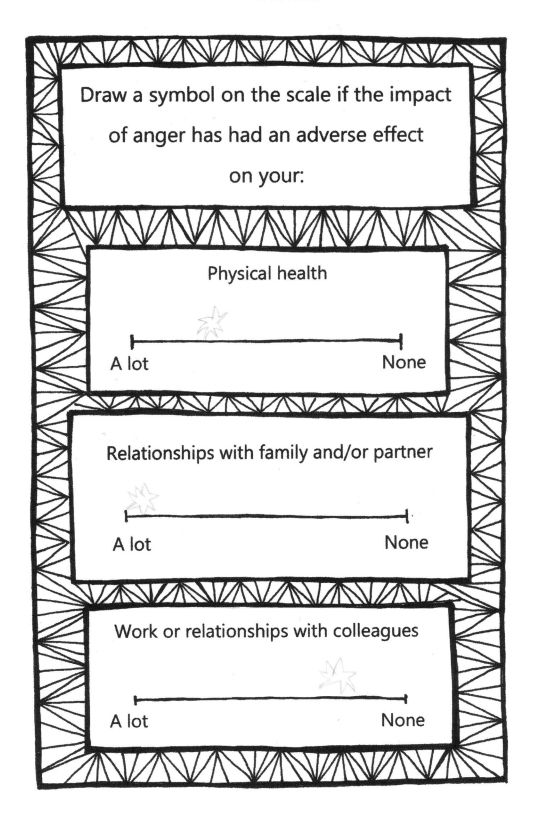

Draw a symbol on the scale if the impact of anger has had an adverse effect on your:

Physical health

A lot · None

Relationships with family and/or partner

A lot · None

Work or relationships with colleagues

A lot · None

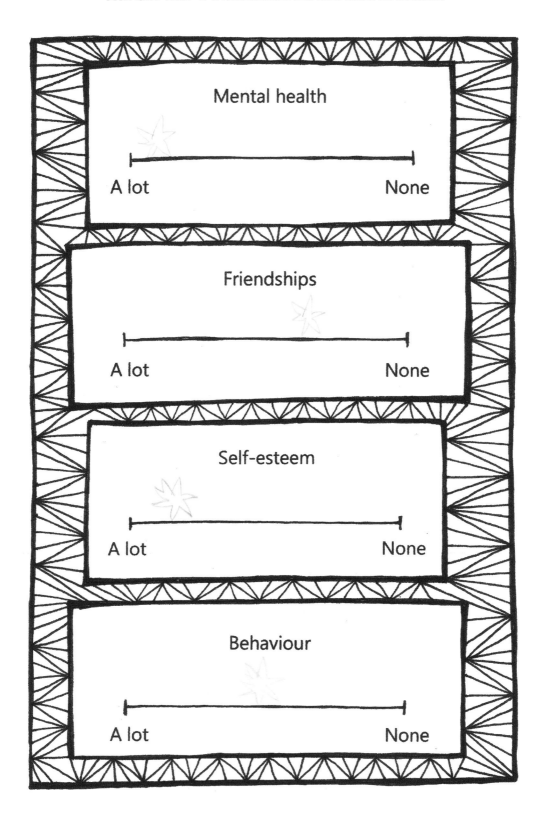

You're not alone

- Almost a third of people say they have a close friend or family member who has trouble controlling their anger

- More than one in ten say that they have trouble controlling their own anger

- More than one in four people say that they worry about how angry they sometimes feel

- One in five people say that they have ended a relationship or friendship with someone because of how they behaved when they were angry

(Myles and Shafran 2015, p.69)

What causes anger?

'Anger is a normal response to threat that helps us defend ourselves if we are under attack and can thus be vital to ensuring our survival. However, too much anger is always counter-productive.'

(Myles and Shafran 2015, p.66)

The threat or attack may be about:

- Physical harm or danger
- Ridicule or criticism
- Harm to others
- Loss or bereavement
- Damage or theft of property or possessions

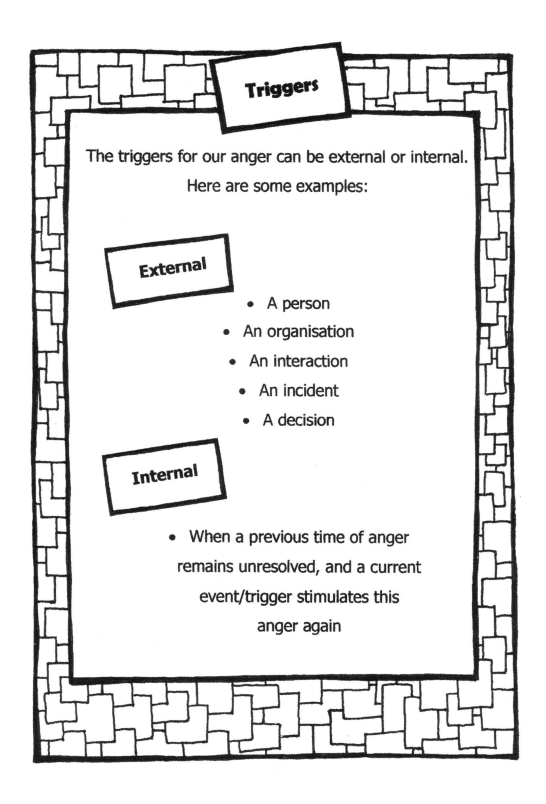

Triggers

The triggers for our anger can be external or internal.
Here are some examples:

External

- A person
- An organisation
- An interaction
- An incident
- A decision

Internal

- When a previous time of anger
  remains unresolved, and a current
  event/trigger stimulates this
  anger again

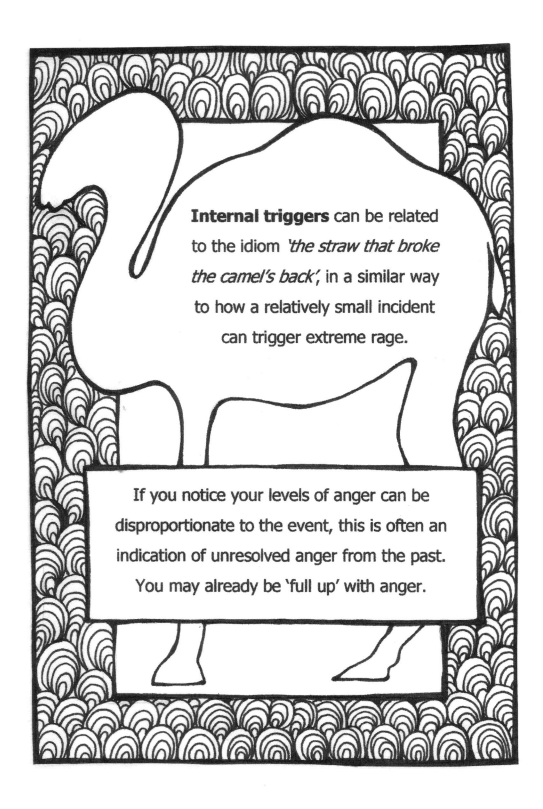

Internal triggers can be related to the idiom *'the straw that broke the camel's back'*, in a similar way to how a relatively small incident can trigger extreme rage.

If you notice your levels of anger can be disproportionate to the event, this is often an indication of unresolved anger from the past. You may already be 'full up' with anger.

Unresolved anger from the past can feel a like how a pressure cooker works. At boiling point the water can bubble over, spill out uncontrollably or may even blow the lid off. In a similar way to regularly releasing a little pressure from the cooker, letting anger out on an ongoing basis can help prevent you feeling like you're reaching 'boiling point' when you may explode or become overwhelmed.

Helpful ways to resolve anger on an ongoing basis:

- Increase our understanding of triggers
- Explore our thoughts, beliefs and meanings we give to events/triggers
- Learn to acknowledge and express our feelings in a safe and calm way

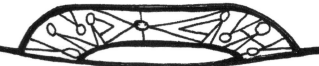

Do you feel as if you're carrying a lot of unresolved anger? On the following page, draw what size container would be big enough to carry away this anger.

Examples are:

- An envelope
- A rucksack
- A recycling box
- A car
- A lorry
- A ship

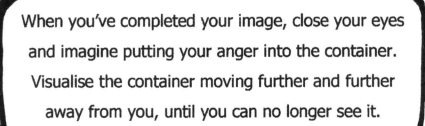

When you've completed your image, close your eyes and imagine putting your anger into the container. Visualise the container moving further and further away from you, until you can no longer see it.

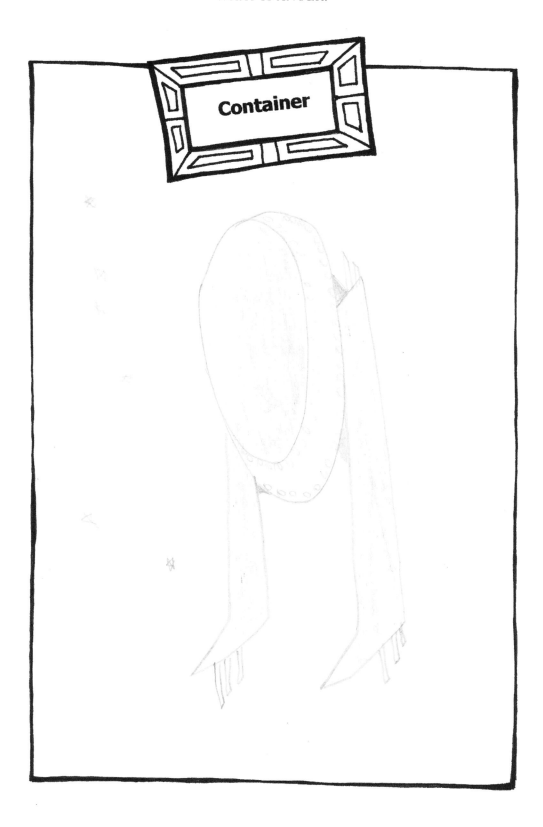

Container

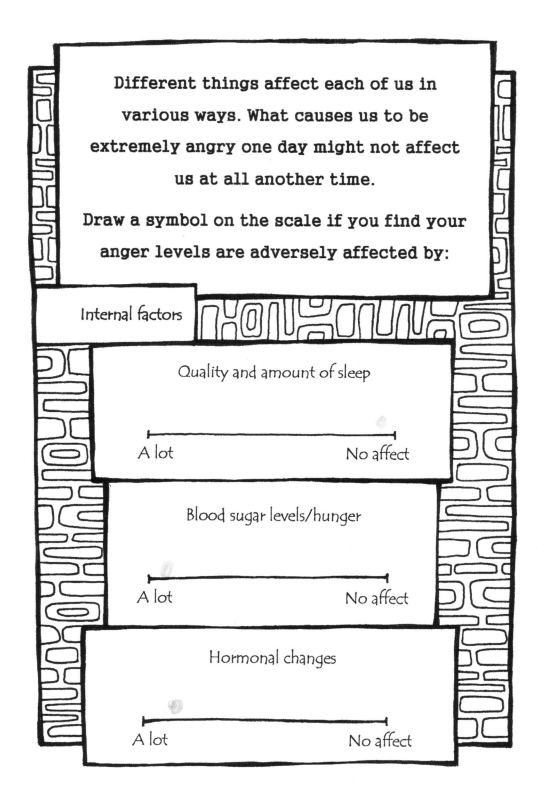

Different things affect each of us in various ways. What causes us to be extremely angry one day might not affect us at all another time.

Draw a symbol on the scale if you find your anger levels are adversely affected by:

Internal factors

Quality and amount of sleep

A lot — No affect

Blood sugar levels/hunger

A lot — No affect

Hormonal changes

A lot — No affect

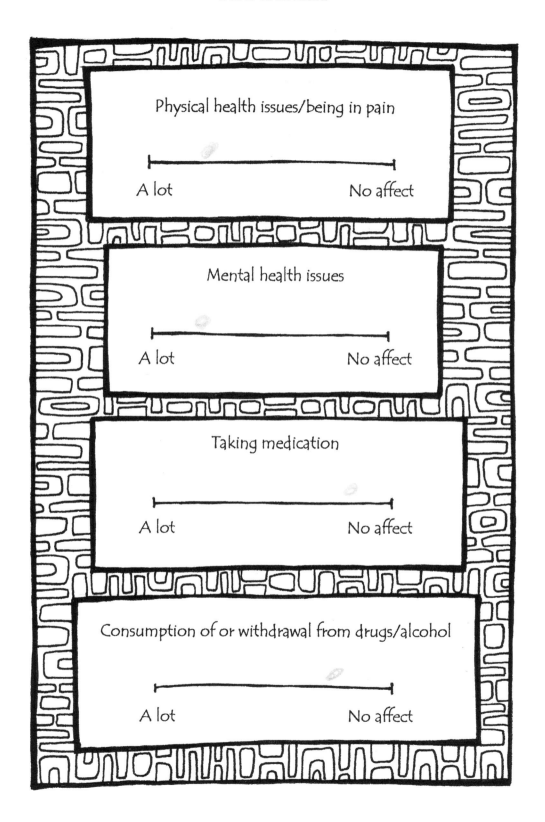

Physical health issues/being in pain

A lot   No affect

Mental health issues

A lot   No affect

Taking medication

A lot   No affect

Consumption of or withdrawal from drugs/alcohol

A lot   No affect

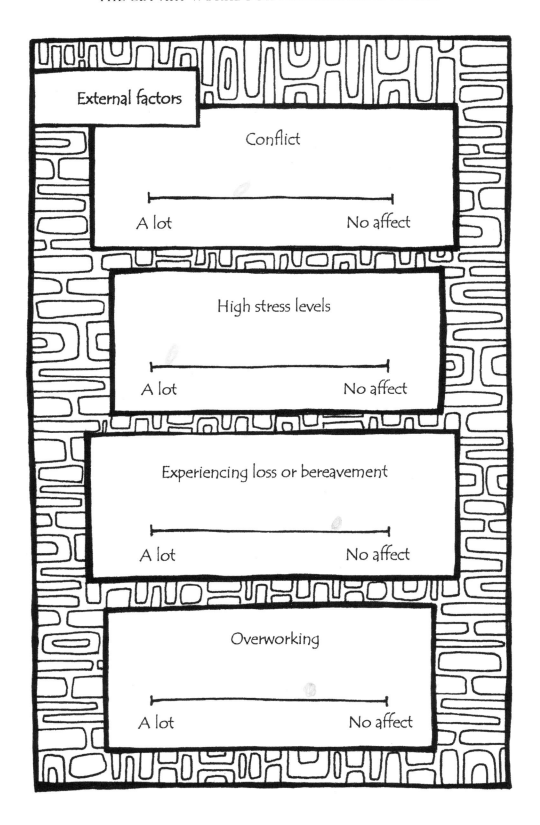

External factors

Conflict

A lot   No affect

High stress levels

A lot   No affect

Experiencing loss or bereavement

A lot   No affect

Overworking

A lot   No affect

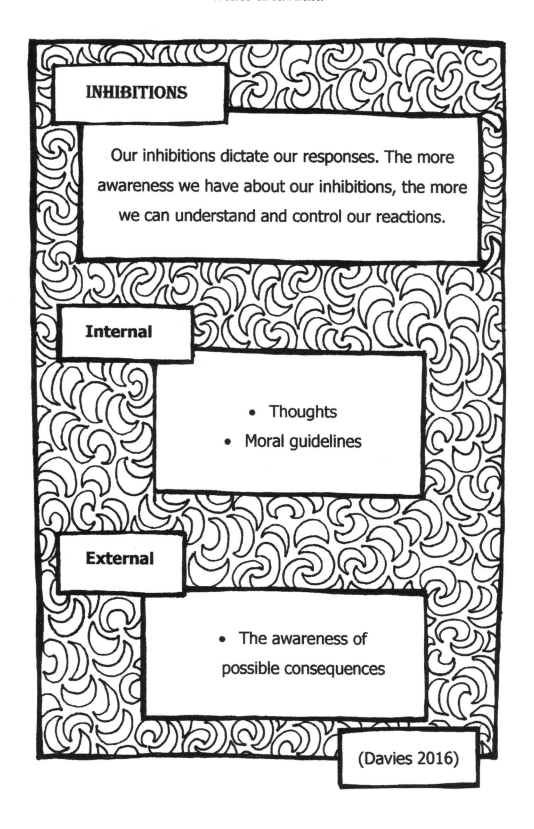

INHIBITIONS

Our inhibitions dictate our responses. The more awareness we have about our inhibitions, the more we can understand and control our reactions.

Internal

- Thoughts
- Moral guidelines

External

- The awareness of possible consequences

(Davies 2016)

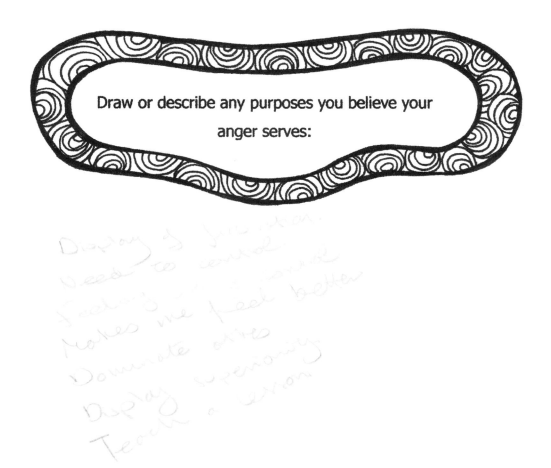

Draw or describe any purposes you believe your anger serves:

Display of frustration.
Need to control
Feeling of power
Makes me feel better
Dominate others
Display superiority
Teach a lesson

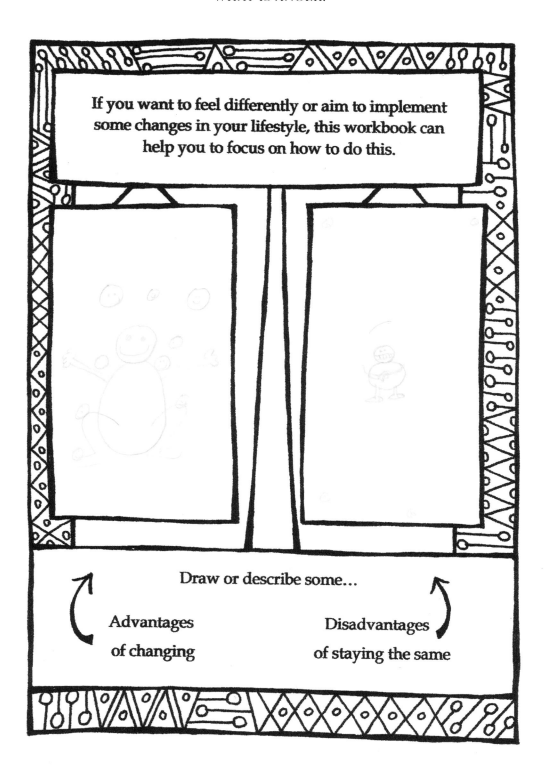

If you want to feel differently or aim to implement some changes in your lifestyle, this workbook can help you to focus on how to do this.

Draw or describe some...

Advantages
of changing

Disadvantages
of staying the same

2

What Is CBT?

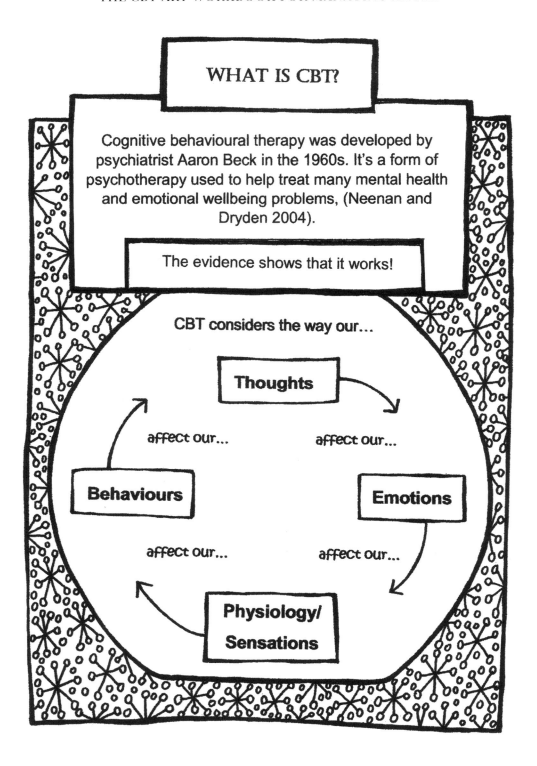

WHAT IS CBT?

Cognitive behavioural therapy was developed by psychiatrist Aaron Beck in the 1960s. It's a form of psychotherapy used to help treat many mental health and emotional wellbeing problems, (Neenan and Dryden 2004).

The evidence shows that it works!

CBT considers the way our...

Thoughts

affect our...

affect our...

Behaviours

Emotions

affect our...

affect our...

Physiology/ Sensations

'The aim of CBT techniques is to disrupt negative thought patterns, so they no longer arouse unbearable emotions.

Recognising thoughts as "just thoughts", rather than mistaking them for true perceptions or impulses that must be acted on, produces a calmer, more positive state of mind.'

(Barford 2018, p.35)

'Studies show that anger responds well to CBT. Many people who experience anger problems see improvements while using appropriate self-help materials.'

(Myles and Shafran 2015, p.77)

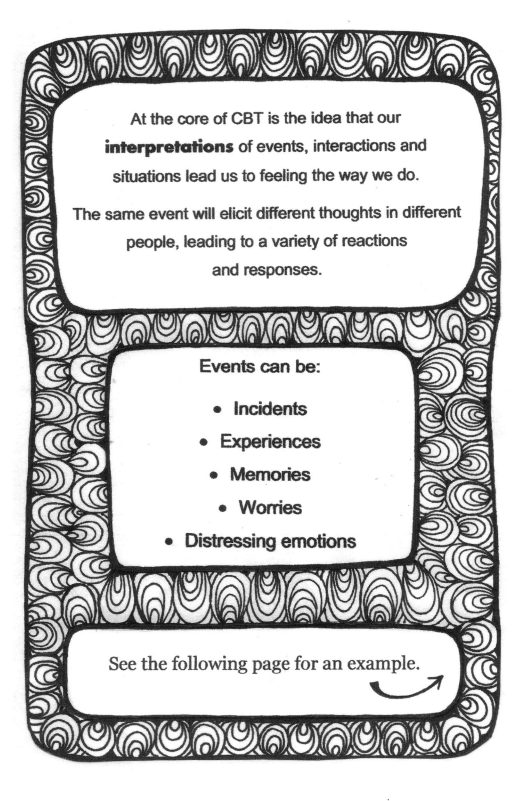

At the core of CBT is the idea that our **interpretations** of events, interactions and situations lead us to feeling the way we do.

The same event will elicit different thoughts in different people, leading to a variety of reactions and responses.

Events can be:

- Incidents
- Experiences
- Memories
- Worries
- Distressing emotions

See the following page for an example.

Example

A friend borrows some money from **Person A**. They promise to return the money at the end of the month. Then they receive an unexpected bill and ask if they can leave it another month to repay it. **Person A** doesn't have much spare cash and at the end of the next month the money isn't returned. **Person A** finds out from someone else that the friend has booked themselves a holiday.

Person A believes the friend is taking advantage of them, thinking that the friend doesn't care about **Person A** or returning their money.

Colour in the symbol to show how this might affect the level of anger **Person A** experiences:

Decrease

Stay the same

Increase

This same scenario happens to **Person B**.

Person B wonders if the friend has forgotten about the borrowed money and thinks the friend may be upset when they realise it's been forgotten. **Person B** also considers that the friend might not know **Person B's** financial situation and how they don't have much spare cash.

Colour in the symbol to show how this is going to impact the level of anger **Person B** experiences:

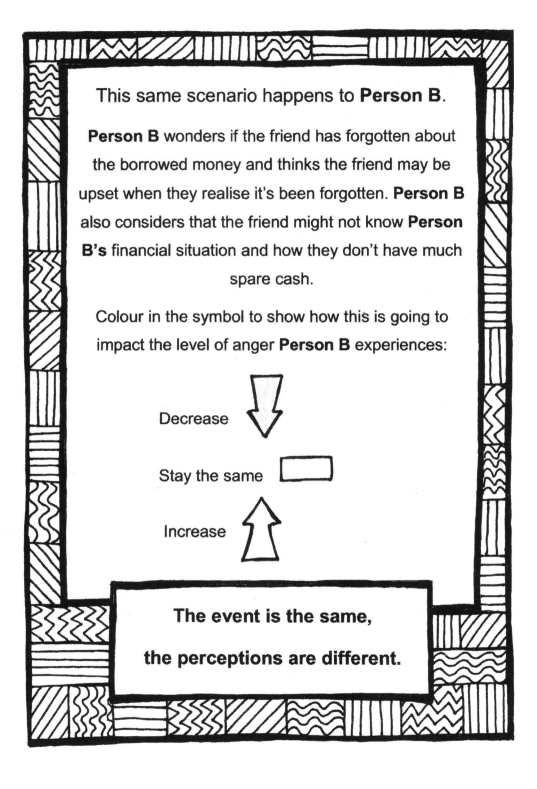

Decrease

Stay the same

Increase

The event is the same,

the perceptions are different.

3

Observations

1. OBSERVATIONS

One of the first techniques used in CBT focuses on raising awareness of our habits. These are around our thoughts, emotions, actions and physiological sensations.

Recording these in a diary or journal enables us to track these different aspects to help make connections between them. Keeping a diary also has the benefit of encouraging us to develop a more objective perspective about our problems (Manning and Ridgeway 2016).

The following pages invite you to fill in the dairy for a week, to help identify the times when you experience anger. Continue in a separate notebook if you'd like to record more. You can choose to make drawings, use symbols or describe your responses.

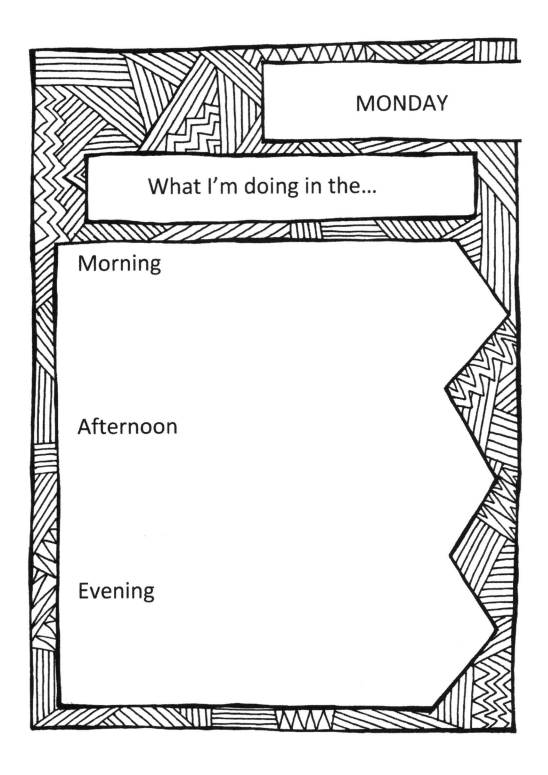

MONDAY

What I'm doing in the...

Morning

Afternoon

Evening

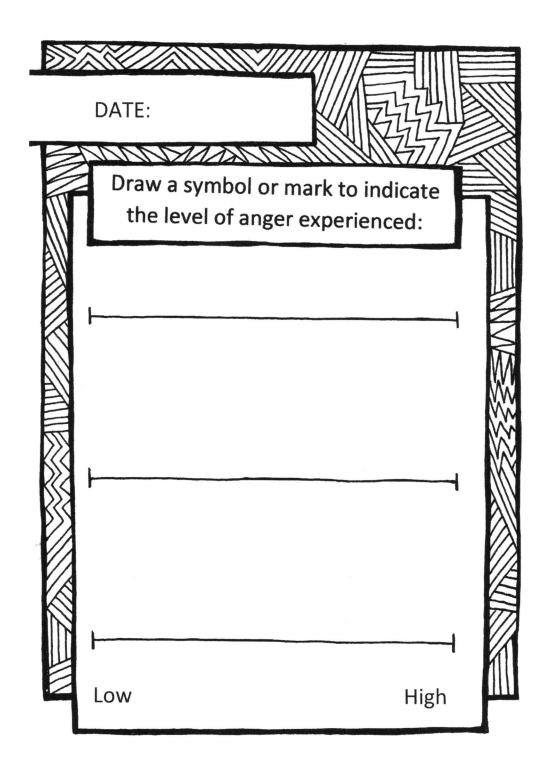

DATE:

Draw a symbol or mark to indicate the level of anger experienced:

Low   High

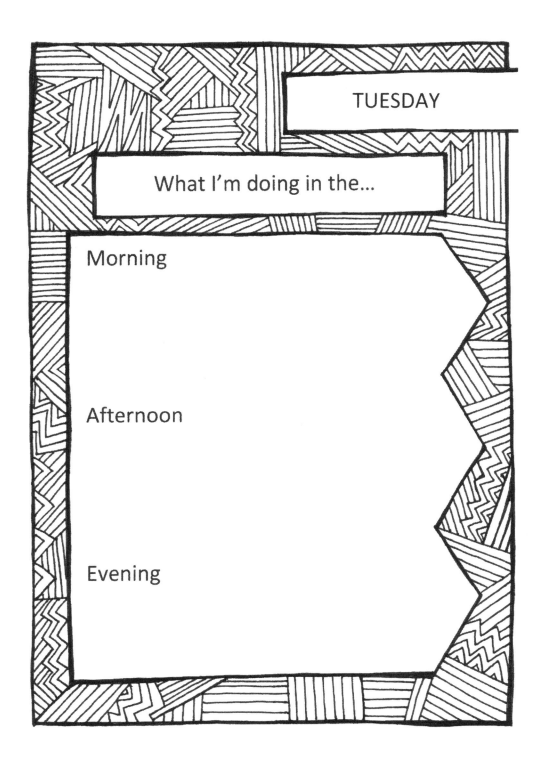

TUESDAY

What I'm doing in the...

Morning

Afternoon

Evening

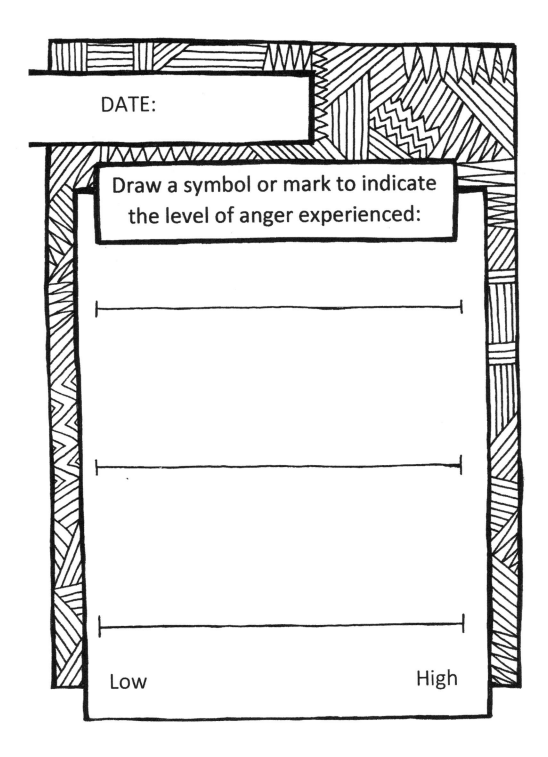

DATE:

Draw a symbol or mark to indicate the level of anger experienced:

⊢————————————⊣

⊢————————————⊣

⊢————————————⊣

Low   High

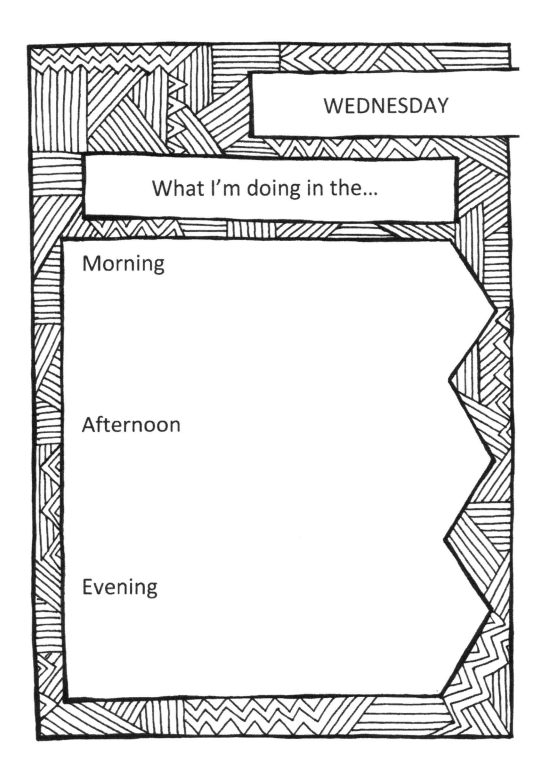

WEDNESDAY

What I'm doing in the...

Morning

Afternoon

Evening

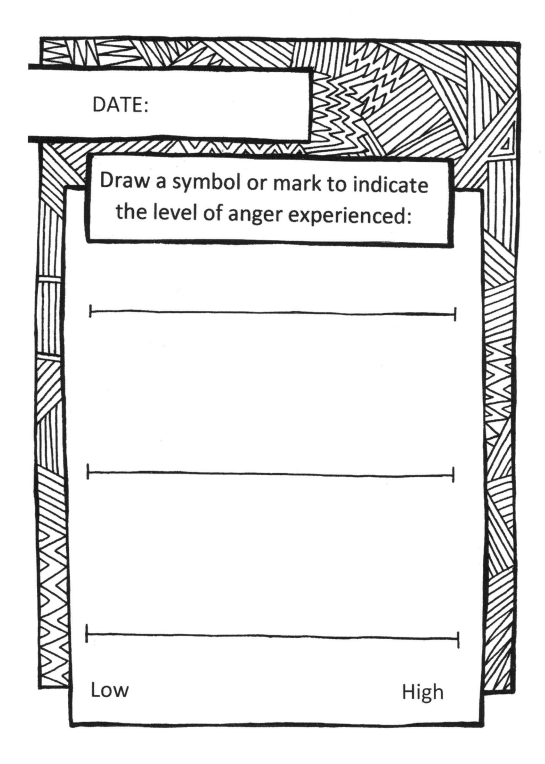

DATE:

Draw a symbol or mark to indicate
the level of anger experienced:

Low   High

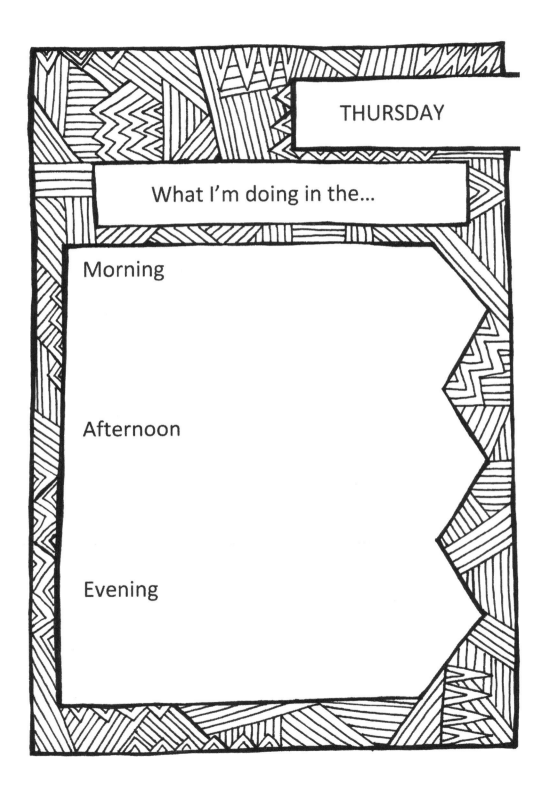

THURSDAY

What I'm doing in the...

Morning

Afternoon

Evening

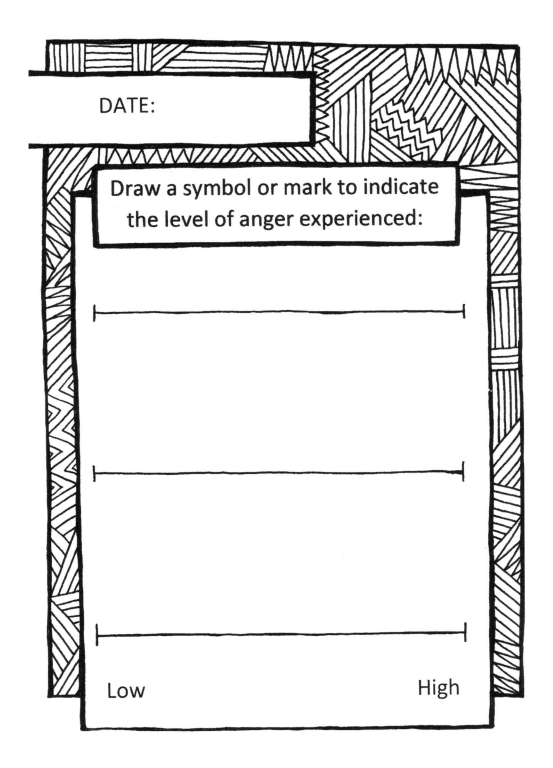

DATE:

Draw a symbol or mark to indicate the level of anger experienced:

Low   High

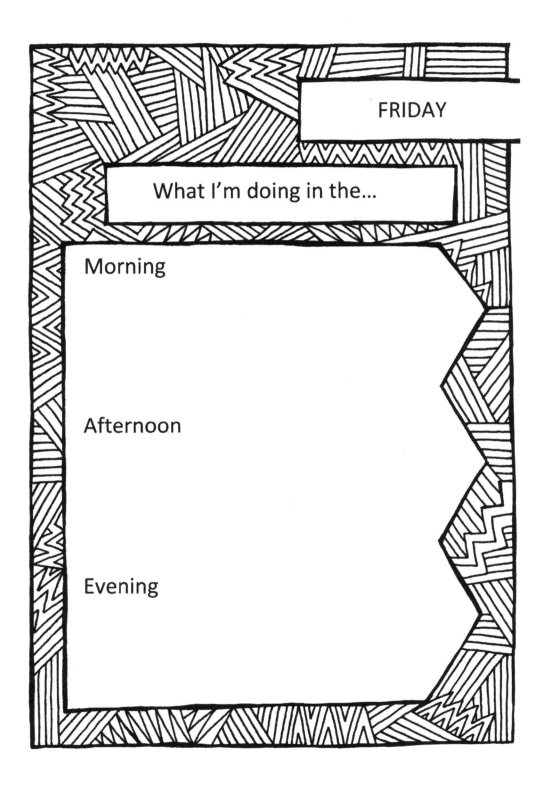

FRIDAY

What I'm doing in the...

Morning

Afternoon

Evening

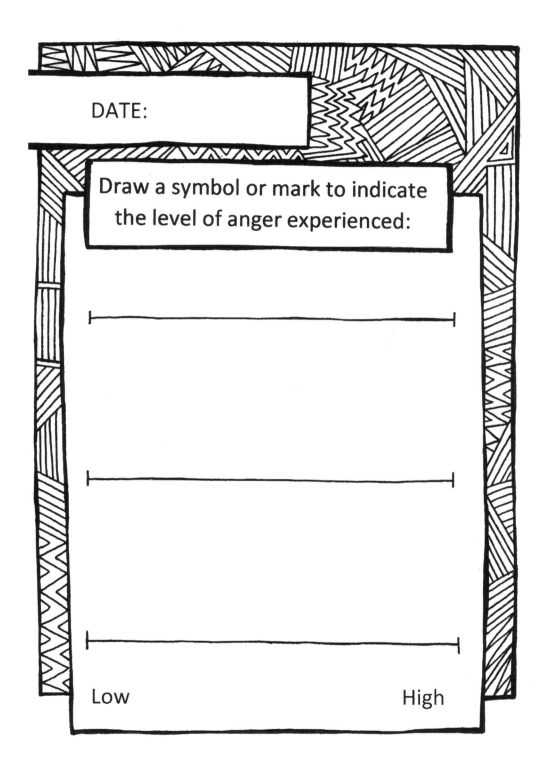

DATE:

Draw a symbol or mark to indicate the level of anger experienced:

Low   High

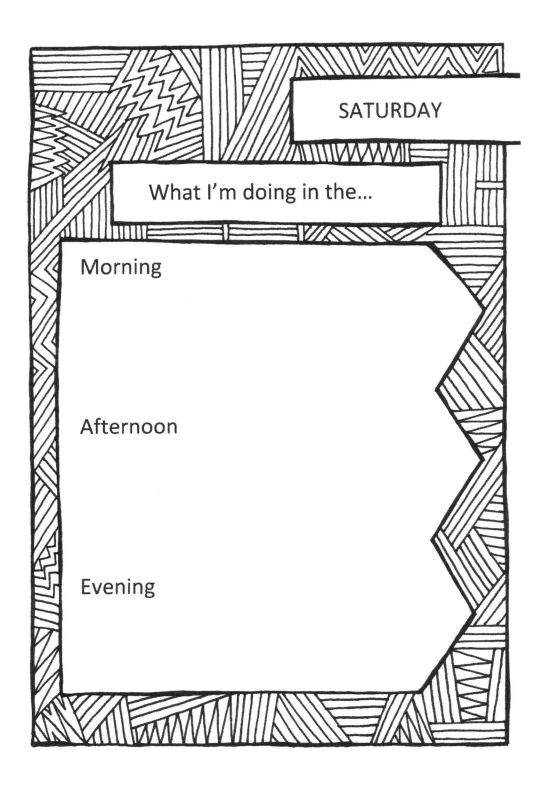

SATURDAY

What I'm doing in the...

Morning

Afternoon

Evening

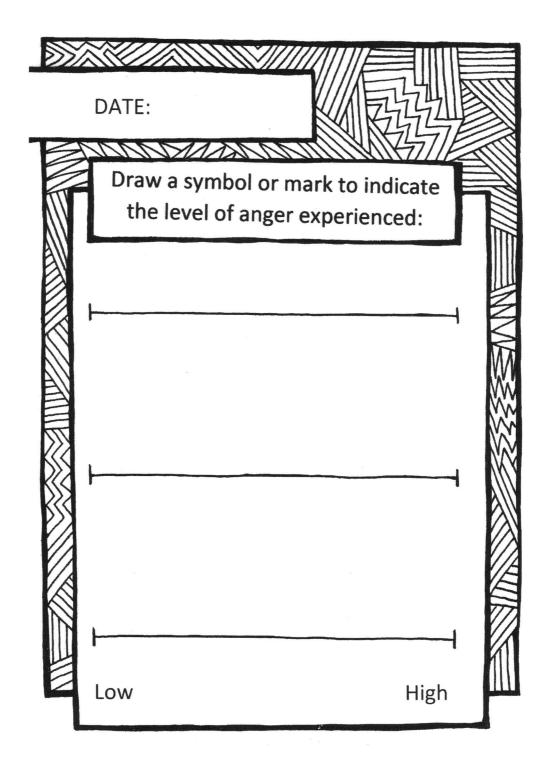

DATE:

Draw a symbol or mark to indicate the level of anger experienced:

Low   High

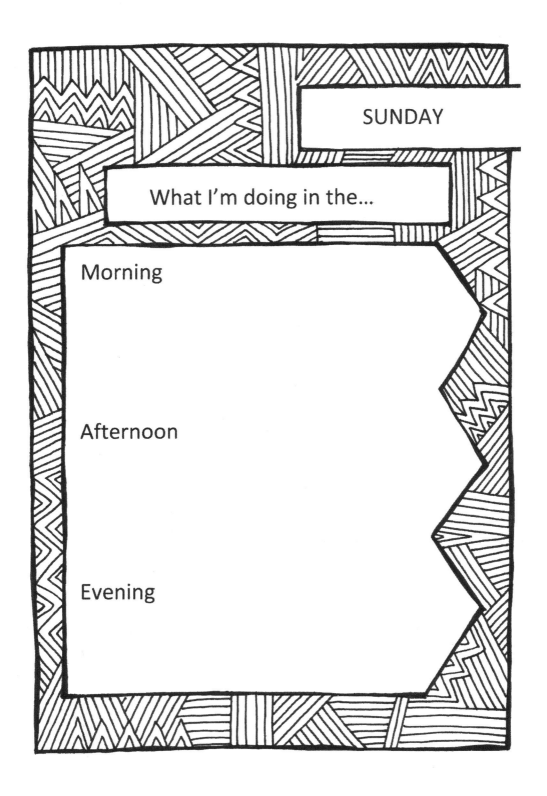

SUNDAY

What I'm doing in the...

Morning

Afternoon

Evening

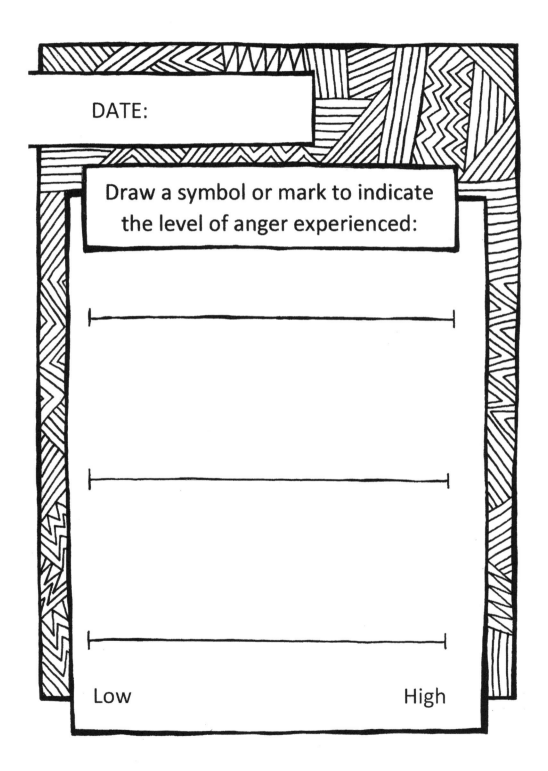

DATE:

Draw a symbol or mark to indicate the level of anger experienced:

Low   High

2. OBSERVATIONS

Once we've identified some situations we find difficult, it's helpful to explore what our…

- Thoughts
- Emotions
- Physiological sensations

…were, to see how these affect our **behaviour**.

We tend to go through our usual day-to-day lives without being very much aware of what our thoughts are about specific things, and how our thinking affects our emotions, mood and behaviour.

Recording some of these helps us to focus on what we want to change, and makes us realise that we can have more control over our emotional and behavioural reactions.

Fill in the following pages with some of the triggering situations when you experience anger.

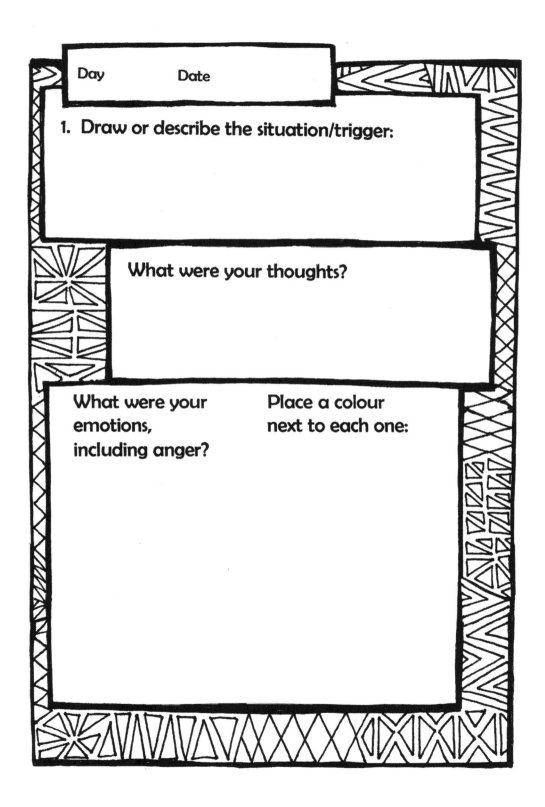

Day   Date

1. Draw or describe the situation/trigger:

What were your thoughts?

What were your   Place a colour
emotions,   next to each one:
including anger?

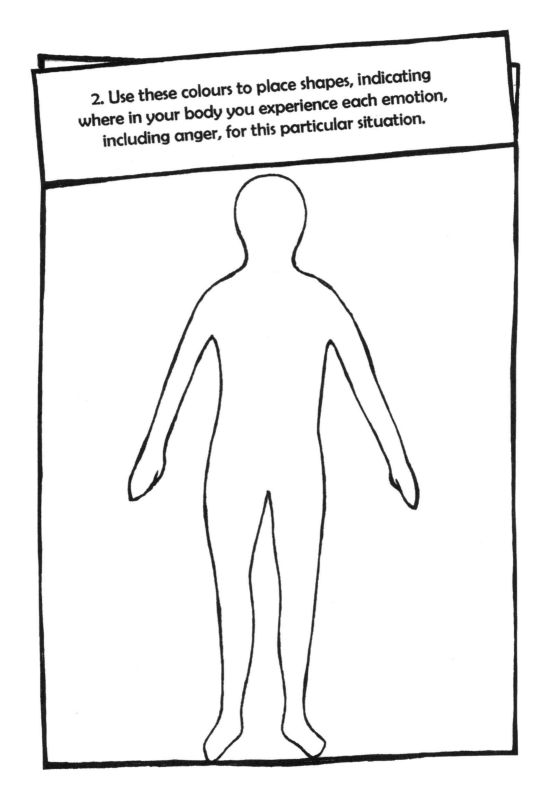

2. Use these colours to place shapes, indicating where in your body you experience each emotion, including anger, for this particular situation.

3. What was your behavioural response?

Draw a symbol on the scale to show how you now feel about your reaction to this event:

Proud ⊢————————————⊣ Regretful

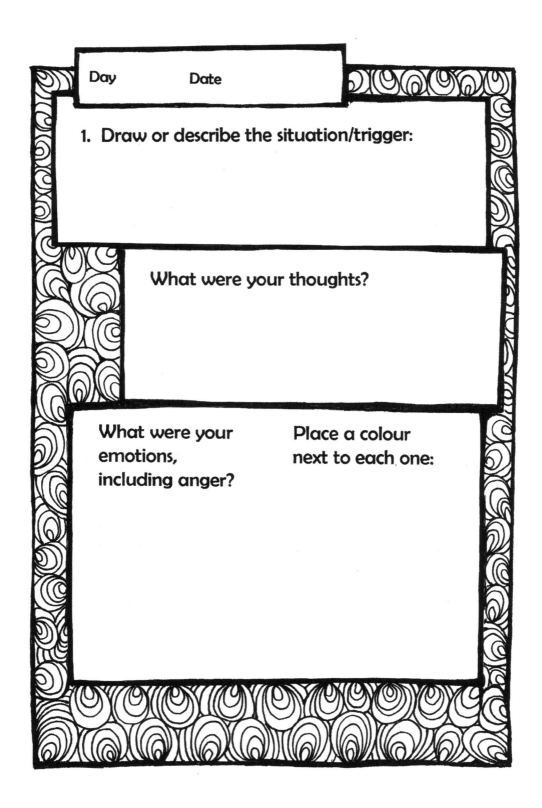

Day   Date

1. Draw or describe the situation/trigger:

What were your thoughts?

What were your   Place a colour
emotions,   next to each one:
including anger?

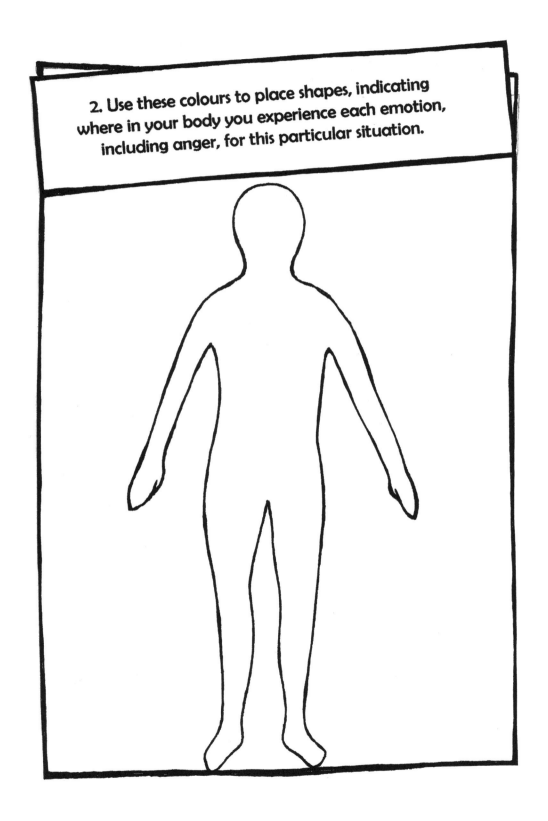

2. Use these colours to place shapes, indicating where in your body you experience each emotion, including anger, for this particular situation.

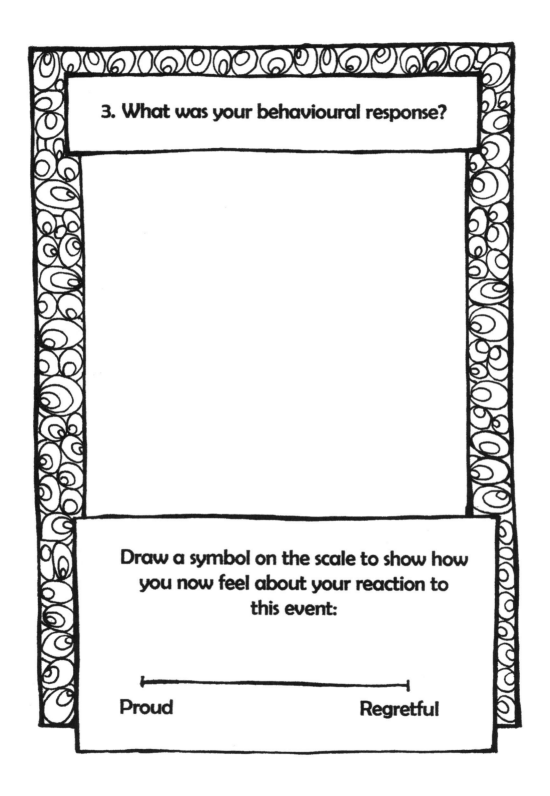

3. What was your behavioural response?

Draw a symbol on the scale to show how you now feel about your reaction to this event:

Proud   Regretful

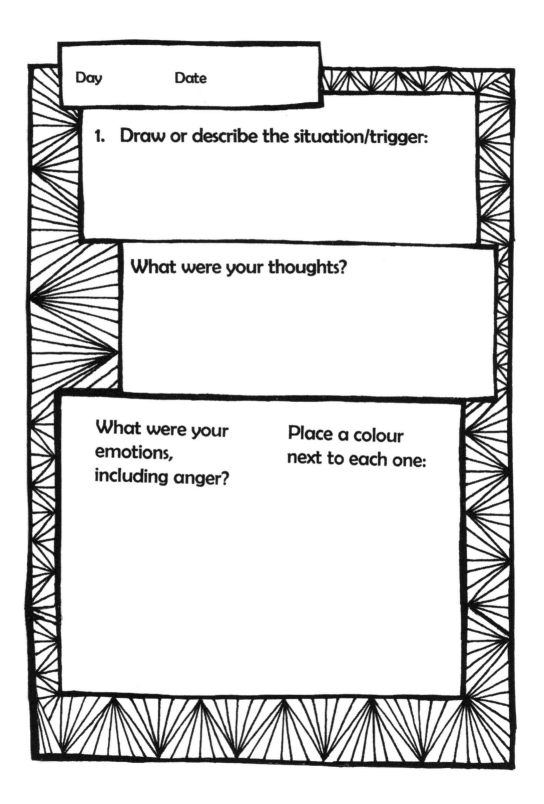

Day   Date

1.   Draw or describe the situation/trigger:

What were your thoughts?

What were your
emotions,
including anger?

Place a colour
next to each one:

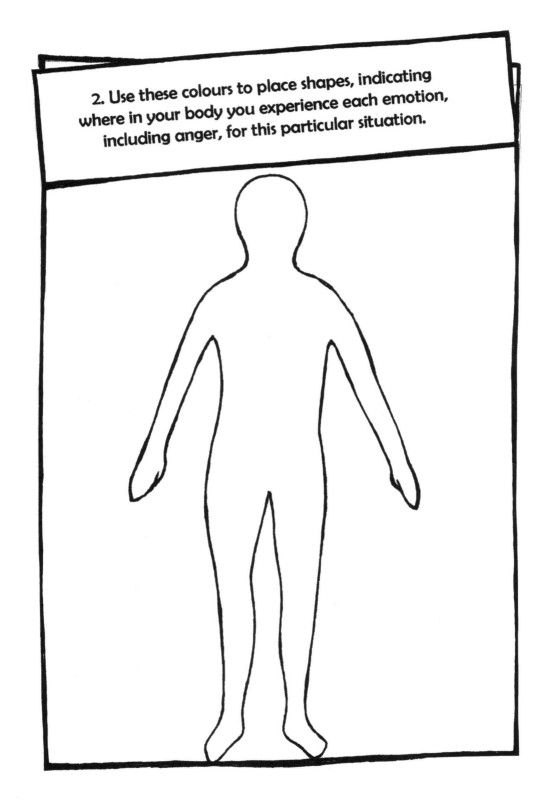

2. Use these colours to place shapes, indicating where in your body you experience each emotion, including anger, for this particular situation.

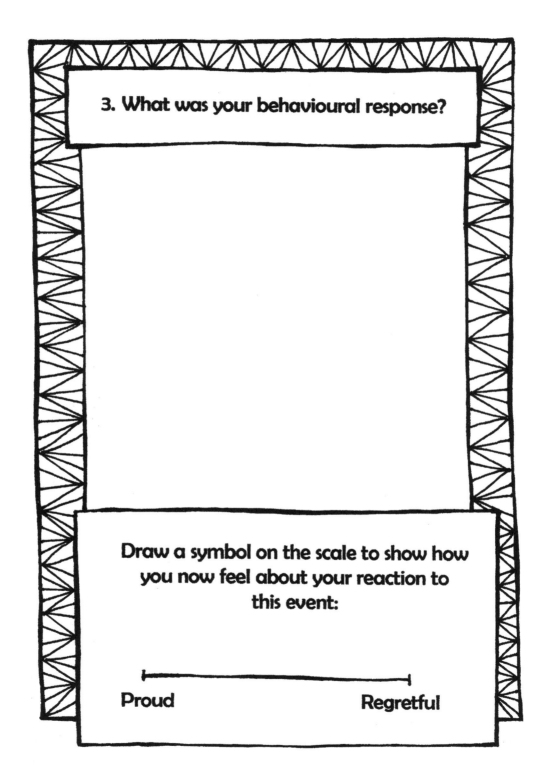

3. What was your behavioural response?

Draw a symbol on the scale to show how you now feel about your reaction to this event:

Proud ————————————————— Regretful

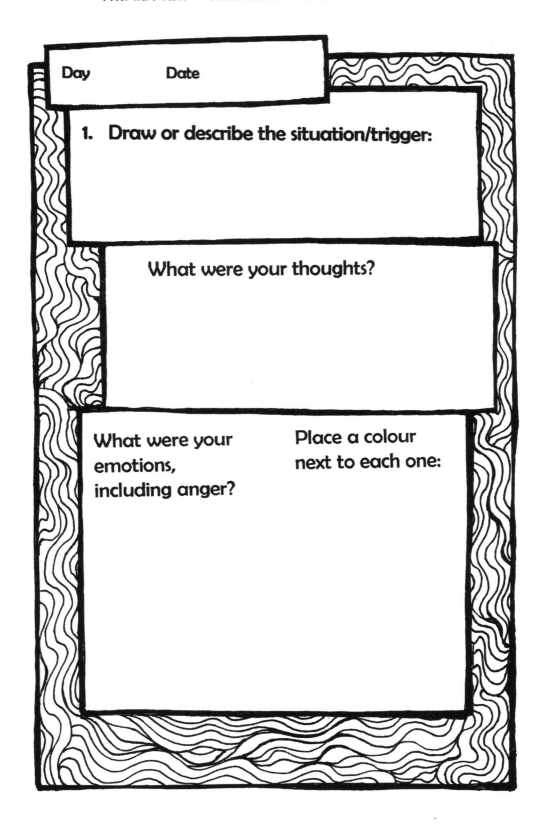

Day   Date

1. Draw or describe the situation/trigger:

What were your thoughts?

What were your
emotions,
including anger?

Place a colour
next to each one:

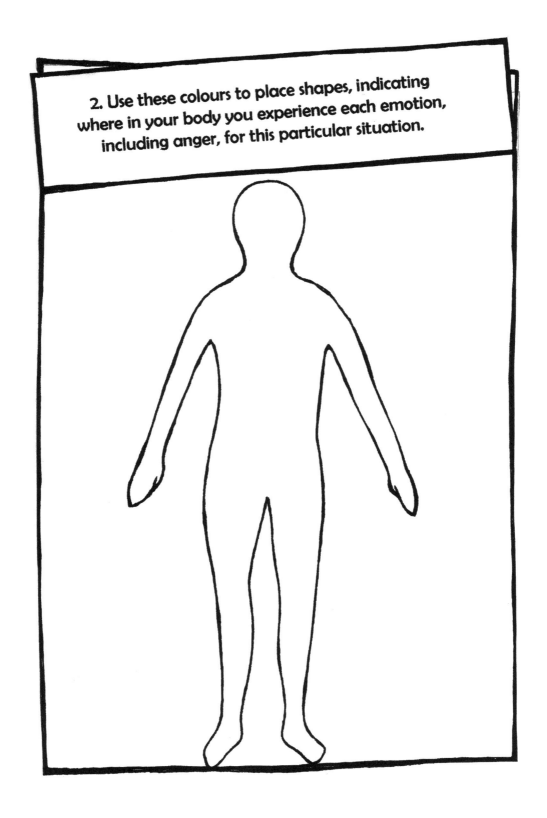

2. Use these colours to place shapes, indicating where in your body you experience each emotion, including anger, for this particular situation.

3. What was your behavioural response?

Draw a symbol on the scale to show how you now feel about your reaction to this event:

Proud   Regretful

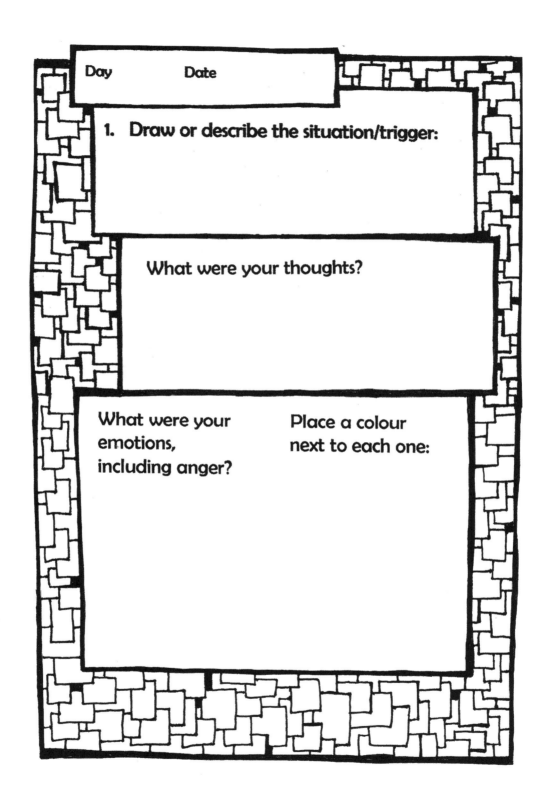

Day   Date

1.   Draw or describe the situation/trigger:

What were your thoughts?

What were your
emotions,
including anger?

Place a colour
next to each one:

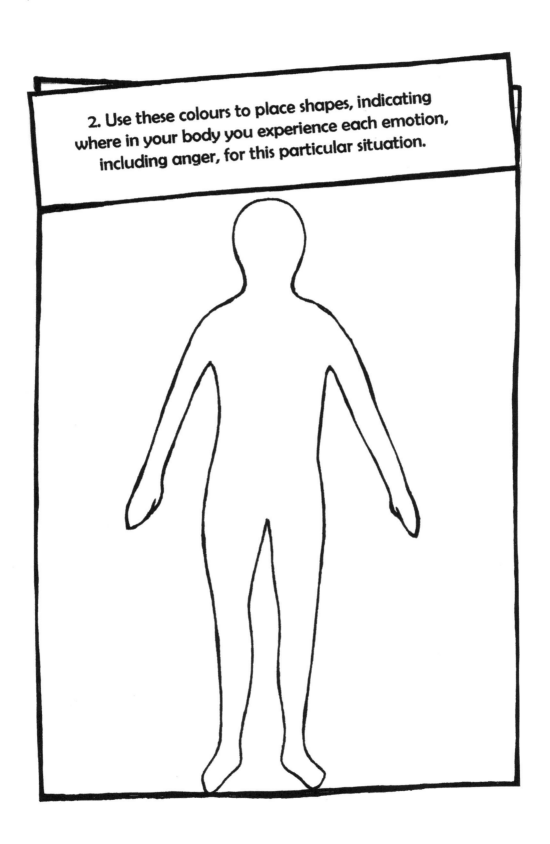

2. Use these colours to place shapes, indicating where in your body you experience each emotion, including anger, for this particular situation.

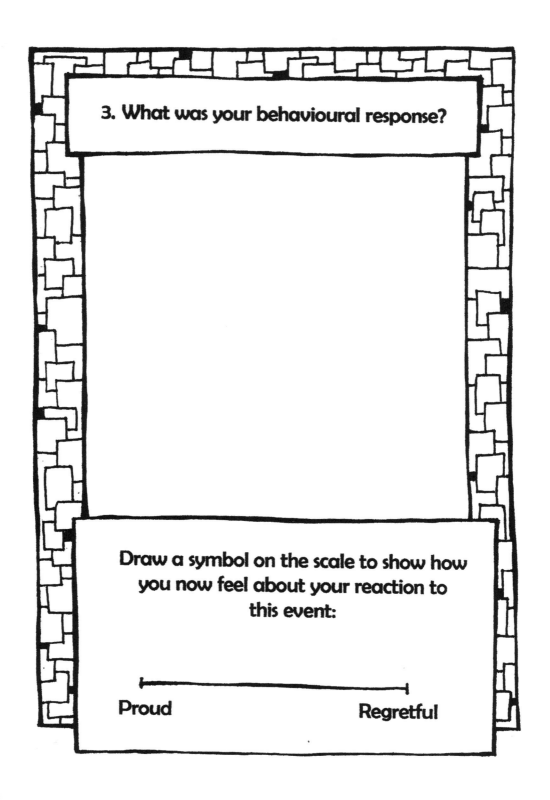

3. What was your behavioural response?

Draw a symbol on the scale to show how you now feel about your reaction to this event:

Proud ————————————————— Regretful

4

Cognitions

COGNITIONS

Colour in the symbols if you often:

Have low concentrations levels

Experience your mind going blank

Think the worst of people

See everything as a big problem

View others as unreasonable

Ruminate over previous experiences of feeling angry

(Maunder *et al.* 2016, pp.9–10)

There are **three different types of thoughts**, some we're more conscious of than others (Beck 1995):

The running commentary, **'self-chatter'** kind of thoughts.

These are called automatic thoughts, are the most superficial, and the ones we're probably aware of the most.

Thoughts that make up our **attitudes** and **assumptions**.

These are the intermediate thoughts, and determine our 'rules', which we're usually only semi-aware of.

Deep-seated thoughts that make up our **beliefs**.

These are our core beliefs, and are the deepest level of thought.

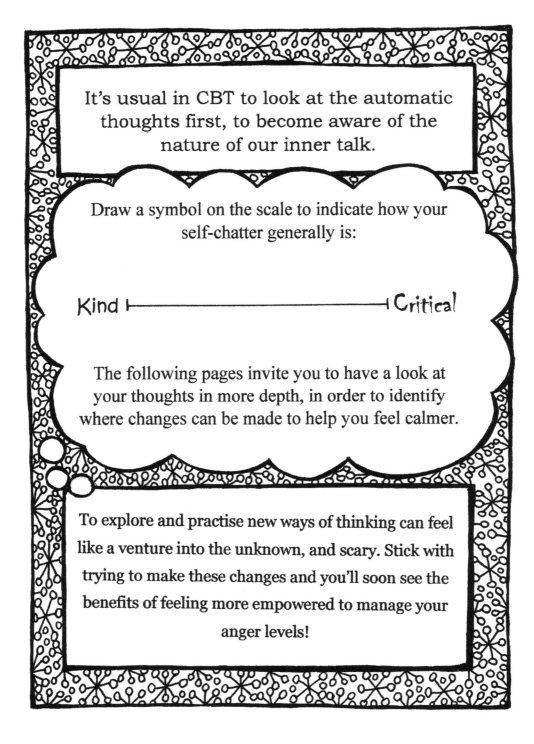

It's usual in CBT to look at the automatic thoughts first, to become aware of the nature of our inner talk.

Draw a symbol on the scale to indicate how your self-chatter generally is:

Kind ├────────────────────┤ Critical

The following pages invite you to have a look at your thoughts in more depth, in order to identify where changes can be made to help you feel calmer.

To explore and practise new ways of thinking can feel like a venture into the unknown, and scary. Stick with trying to make these changes and you'll soon see the benefits of feeling more empowered to manage your anger levels!

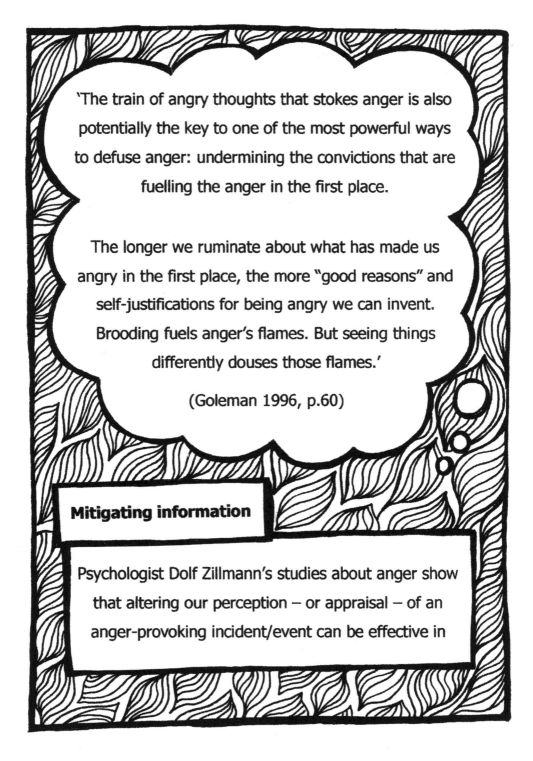

'The train of angry thoughts that stokes anger is also potentially the key to one of the most powerful ways to defuse anger: undermining the convictions that are fuelling the anger in the first place.

The longer we ruminate about what has made us angry in the first place, the more "good reasons" and self-justifications for being angry we can invent. Brooding fuels anger's flames. But seeing things differently douses those flames.'

(Goleman 1996, p.60)

Mitigating information

Psychologist Dolf Zillmann's studies about anger show that altering our perception – or appraisal – of an anger-provoking incident/event can be effective in

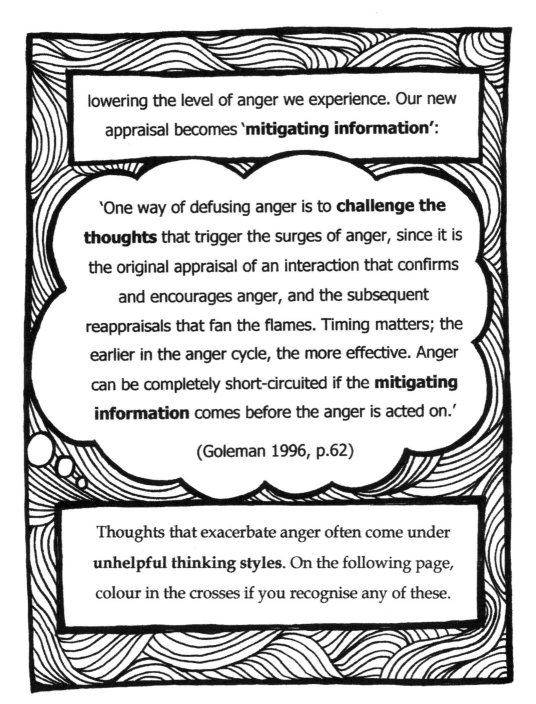

lowering the level of anger we experience. Our new appraisal becomes '**mitigating information**':

'One way of defusing anger is to **challenge the thoughts** that trigger the surges of anger, since it is the original appraisal of an interaction that confirms and encourages anger, and the subsequent reappraisals that fan the flames. Timing matters; the earlier in the anger cycle, the more effective. Anger can be completely short-circuited if the **mitigating information** comes before the anger is acted on.'

(Goleman 1996, p.62)

Thoughts that exacerbate anger often come under **unhelpful thinking styles**. On the following page, colour in the crosses if you recognise any of these.

Do you tend to take things personally and feel hurt by these?

Do you focus your thoughts about negative or bad events and ignore the positive or good ones?

Do you expect too much from yourself and/or those around you?

Do you think rigidly in 'black or white, all or nothing' terms?

Do you have high standards and feel badly let down and hurt if these aren't met?

(Maunder *et al.* 2016, pp.9–10)

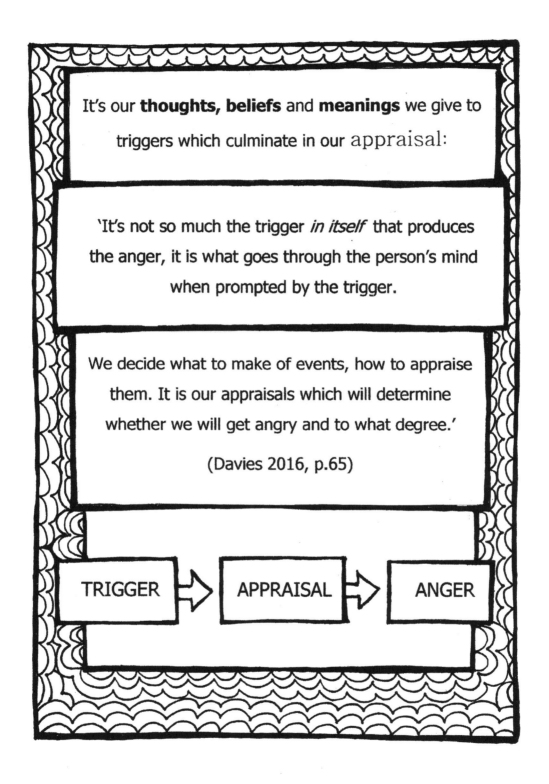

It's our **thoughts, beliefs** and **meanings** we give to triggers which culminate in our appraisal:

'It's not so much the trigger *in itself* that produces the anger, it is what goes through the person's mind when prompted by the trigger.

We decide what to make of events, how to appraise them. It is our appraisals which will determine whether we will get angry and to what degree.'

(Davies 2016, p.65)

TRIGGER ➡ APPRAISAL ➡ ANGER

Psychologist William Davies (2016, p.162) states how

'It is possible to make appraisals that are better for all concerned, making you and other people feel better about the situation.'

He describes some of the best ways to do this:

- Identify negative or hostile thoughts, and try to replace these
- Use the 'friend technique': How would an all-knowing, all-wise friend advise you to view the situation?
- Reframe the situation by searching for good aspects of it or try viewing it from a completely different perspective
- Explore and analyse the costs and benefits of staying the same with your initial appraisal. Is there a more cost-effective perception?

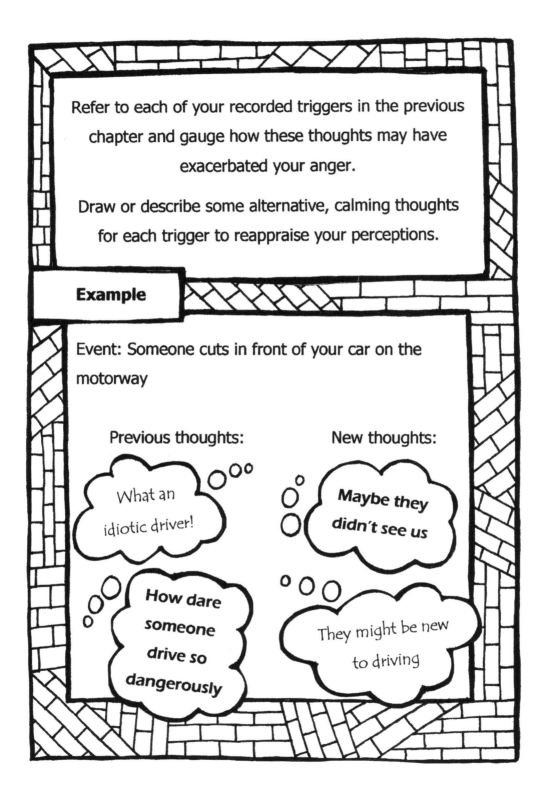

Refer to each of your recorded triggers in the previous chapter and gauge how these thoughts may have exacerbated your anger.

Draw or describe some alternative, calming thoughts for each trigger to reappraise your perceptions.

Example

Event: Someone cuts in front of your car on the motorway

Previous thoughts:

What an idiotic driver!

How dare someone drive so dangerously

New thoughts:

Maybe they didn't see us

They might be new to driving

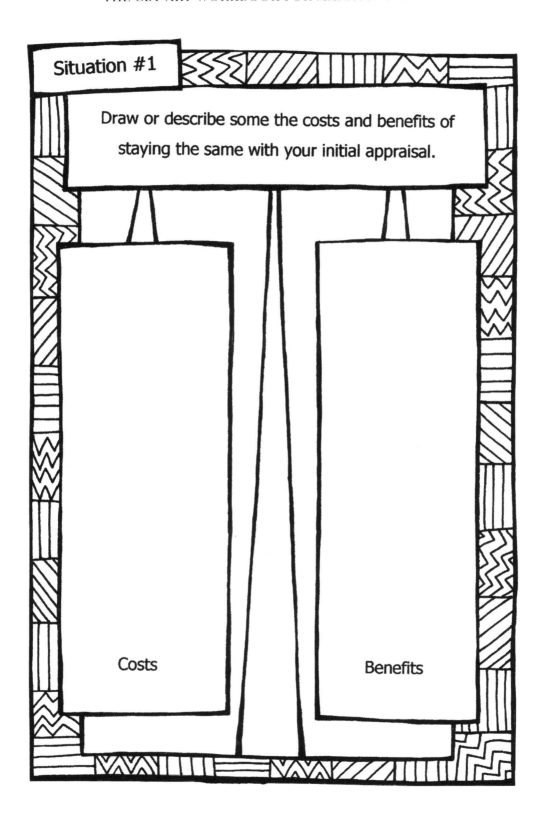

Situation #1

Draw or describe some the costs and benefits of staying the same with your initial appraisal.

Costs

Benefits

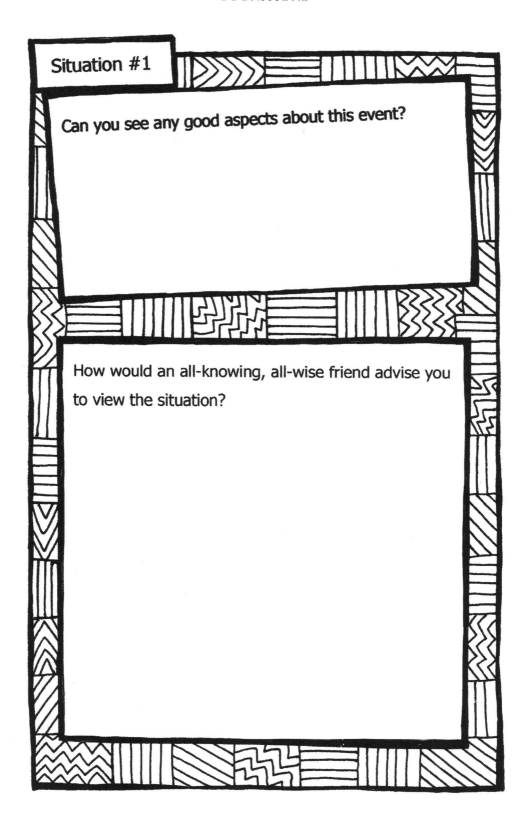

Situation #1

Can you see any good aspects about this event?

How would an all-knowing, all-wise friend advise you to view the situation?

Trigger situation #2

Draw or describe the event:

Previous thoughts:

New thoughts:

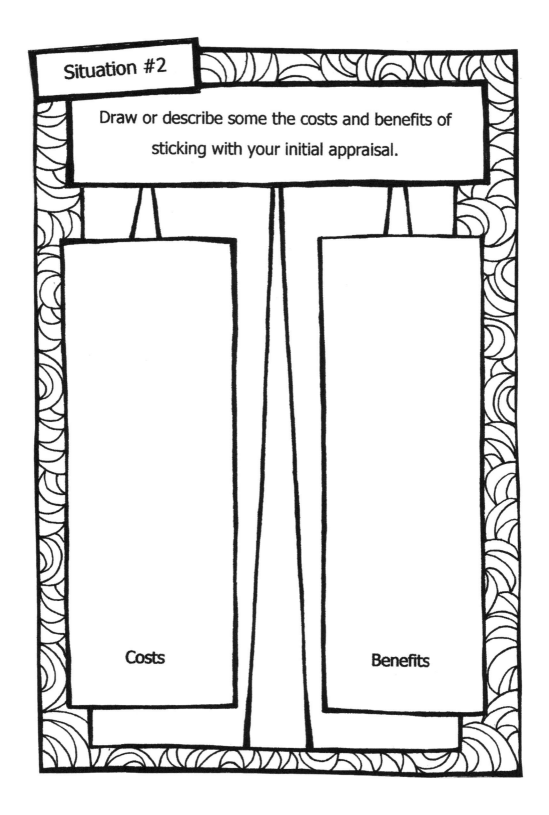

Situation #2

Draw or describe some the costs and benefits of sticking with your initial appraisal.

Costs

Benefits

Situation #2

Can you see any good aspects about this event?

How would an all-knowing, all-wise friend advise you to view the situation?

Trigger situation #3

Draw or describe the event:

Previous thoughts:

New thoughts:

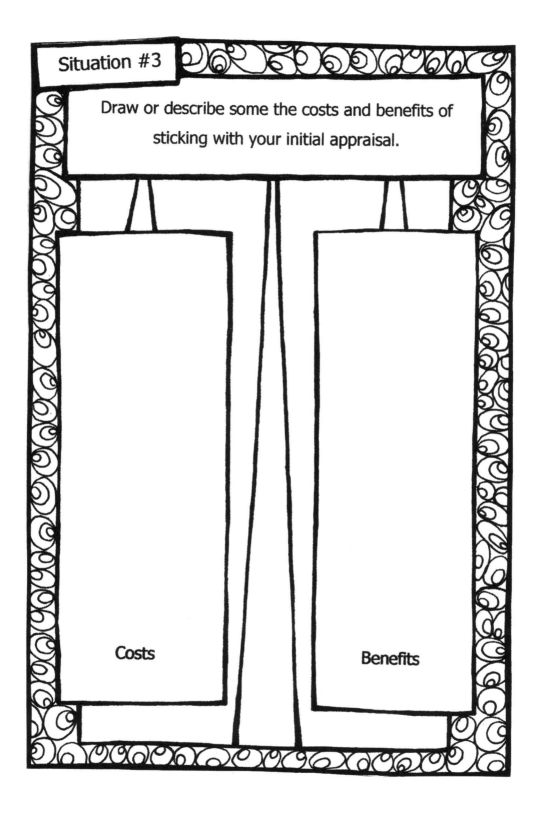

Situation #3

Draw or describe some the costs and benefits of sticking with your initial appraisal.

Costs

Benefits

Situation #3

Can you see any good aspects about this event?

How would an all-knowing, all-wise friend advise you to view the situation?

Trigger situation #4

Draw or describe the event:

Previous thoughts:

New thoughts:

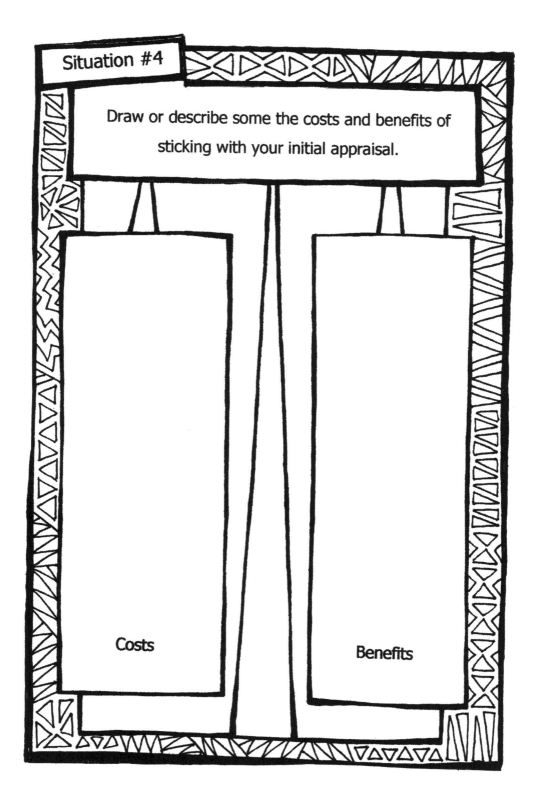

Situation #4

Draw or describe some the costs and benefits of sticking with your initial appraisal.

Costs

Benefits

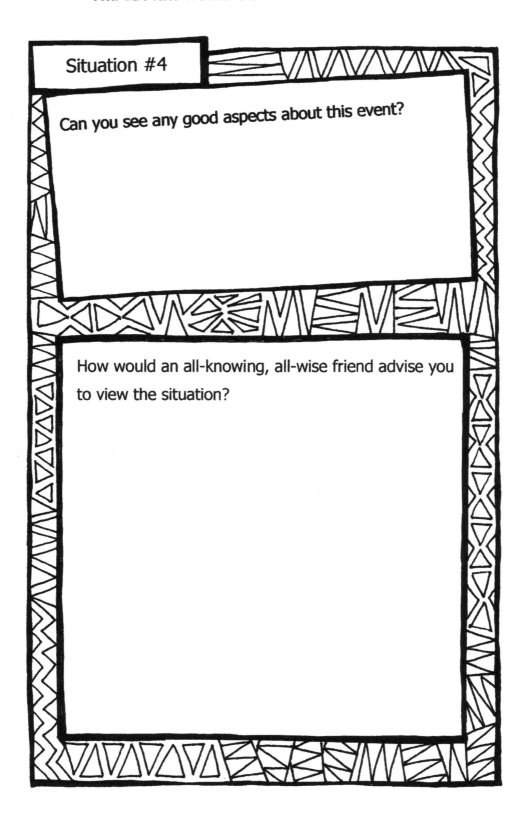

Situation #4

Can you see any good aspects about this event?

How would an all-knowing, all-wise friend advise you to view the situation?

Trigger situation #5

Draw or describe the event:

Previous thoughts:

New thoughts:

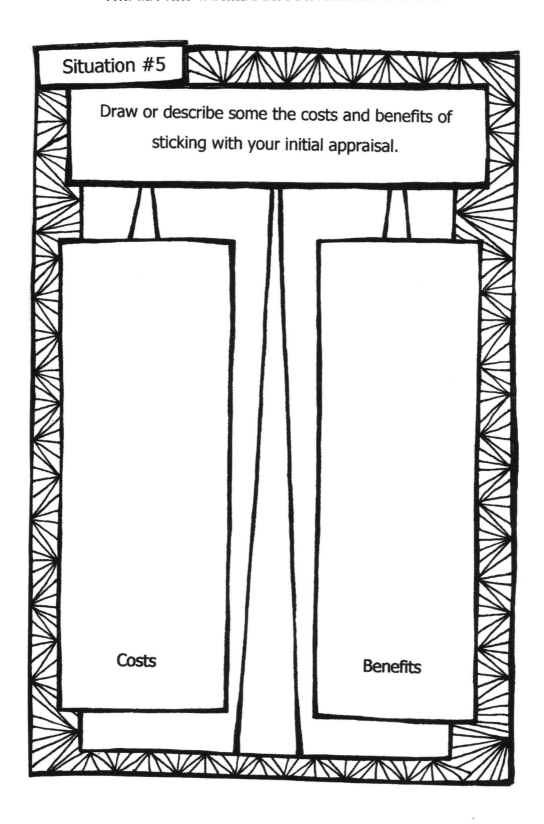

Situation #5

Draw or describe some the costs and benefits of sticking with your initial appraisal.

Costs

Benefits

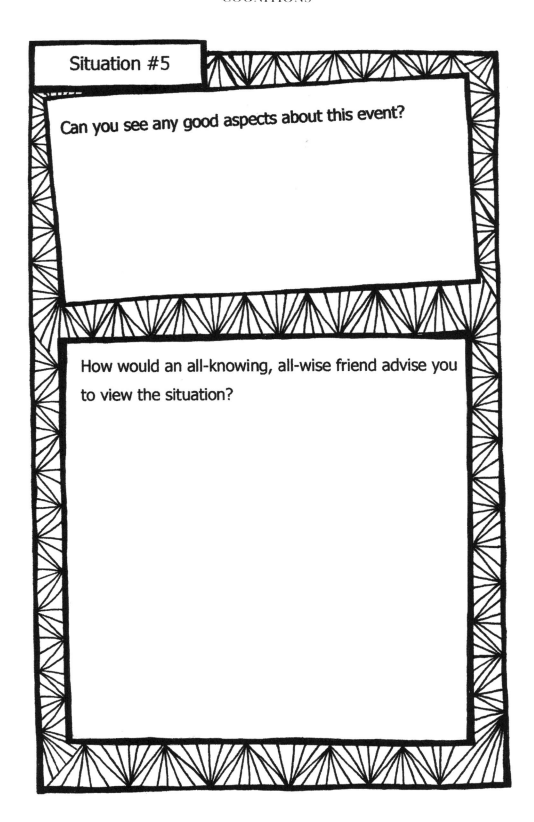

Situation #5

Can you see any good aspects about this event?

How would an all-knowing, all-wise friend advise you to view the situation?

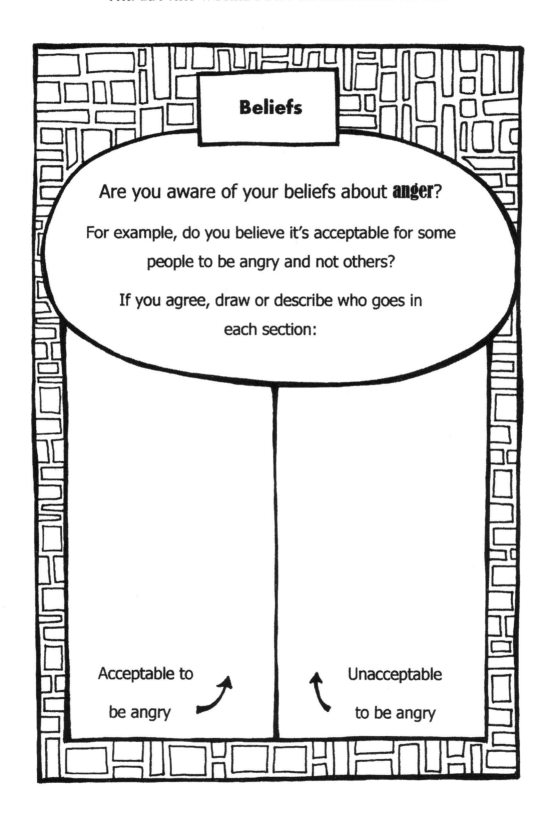

Beliefs

Are you aware of your beliefs about **anger**?

For example, do you believe it's acceptable for some people to be angry and not others?

If you agree, draw or describe who goes in each section:

Acceptable to be angry

Unacceptable to be angry

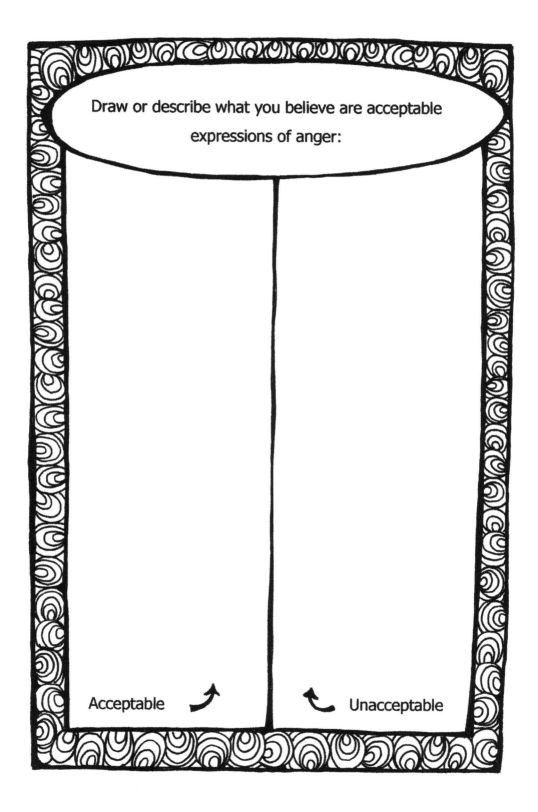

Draw or describe what you believe are acceptable expressions of anger:

Acceptable

Unacceptable

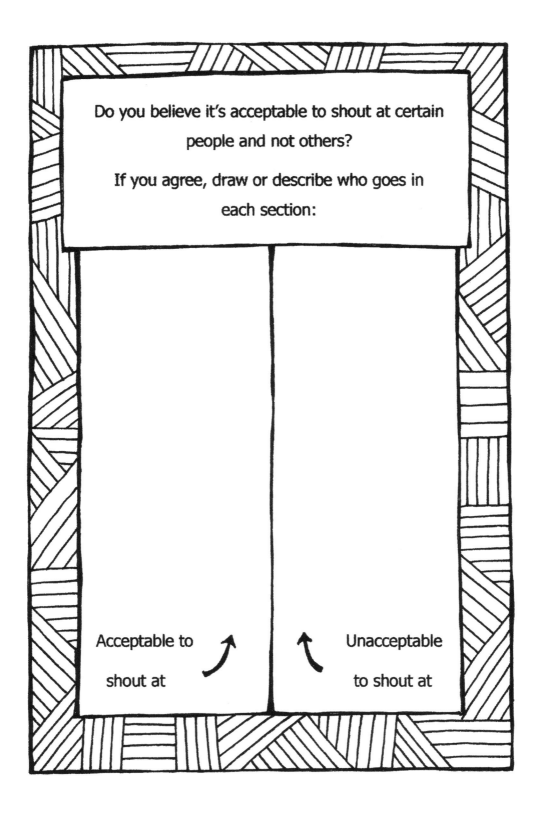

Do you believe it's acceptable to shout at certain people and not others?

If you agree, draw or describe who goes in each section:

Acceptable to shout at

Unacceptable to shout at

Do you believe it's acceptable to react aggressively in some situations and not others? Draw or describe examples of each:

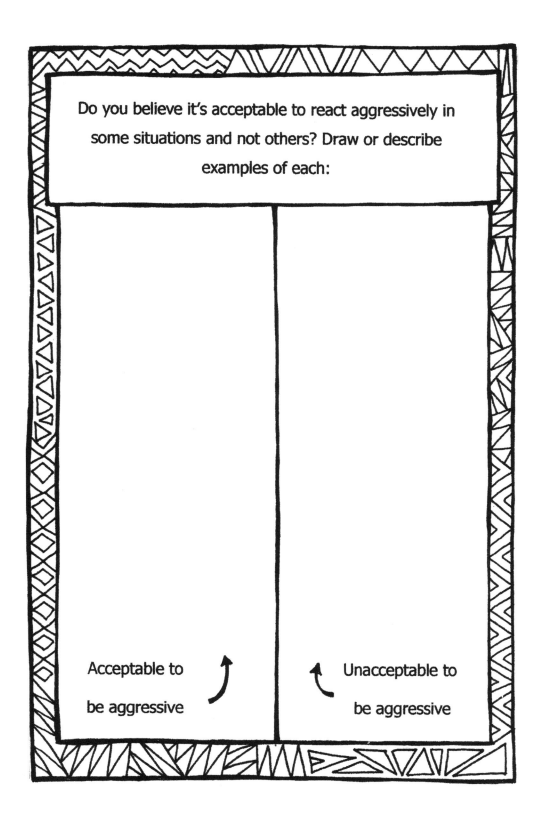

Acceptable to

be aggressive

Unacceptable to

be aggressive

Distraction

'The power of distraction is that it stops that angry train of thought, since each such thought is in itself a minor trigger for more cascades of anger.'

(Goleman 1996, p.63)

Distractions need to be **cognitively engaging** for them to be effective, and provide a 'cooling off' period.

Affirmations

These are **positive** and **self-soothing** statements. As soon as you notice your inner self-talk becoming critical or hostile, replace it with an affirmation, such as the ones on the next few pages.

Try repeating the affirmations over and over again in your mind as you colour in the phrase. The more often you practise, the easier it will be to remember them and you'll be able to more readily access them in future situations to help halt rising levels of anger.

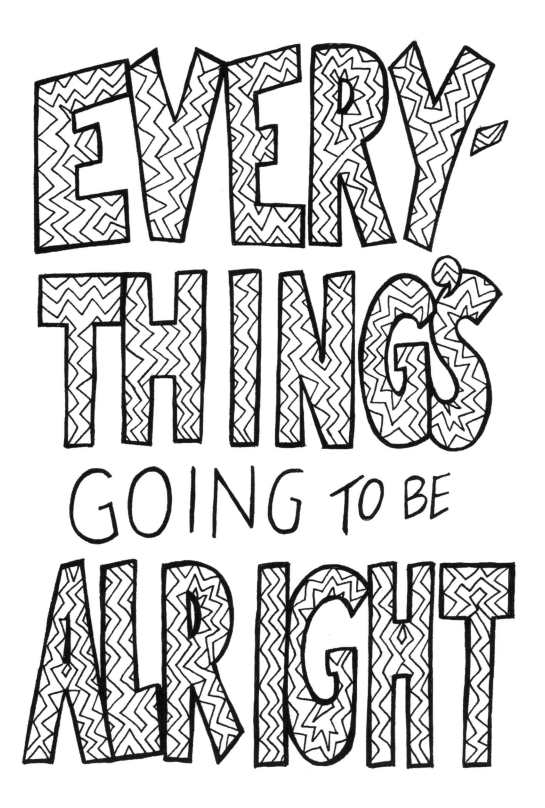

5

Emotions

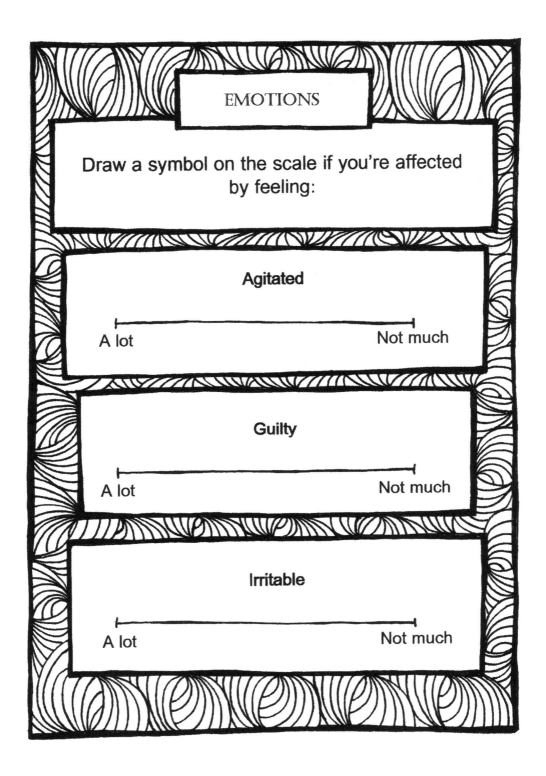

EMOTIONS

Draw a symbol on the scale if you're affected by feeling:

Agitated

A lot —————————————————— Not much

Guilty

A lot —————————————————— Not much

Irritable

A lot —————————————————— Not much

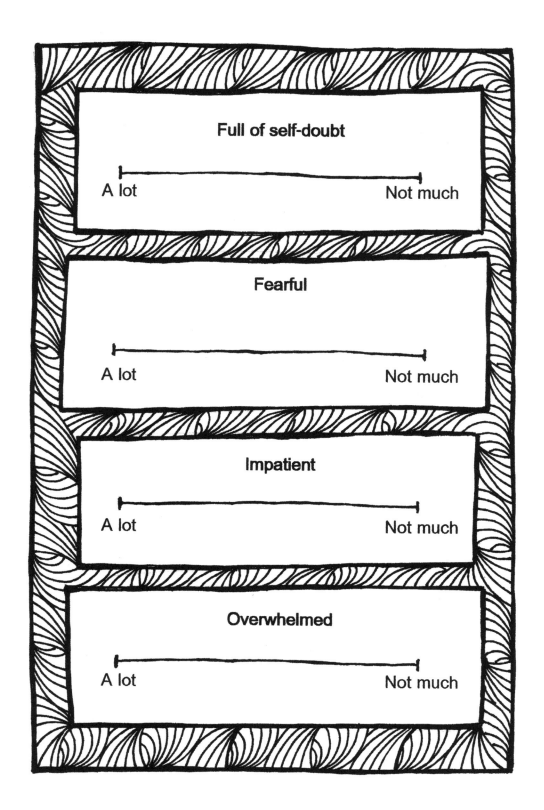

Full of self-doubt

A lot   Not much

Fearful

A lot   Not much

Impatient

A lot   Not much

Overwhelmed

A lot   Not much

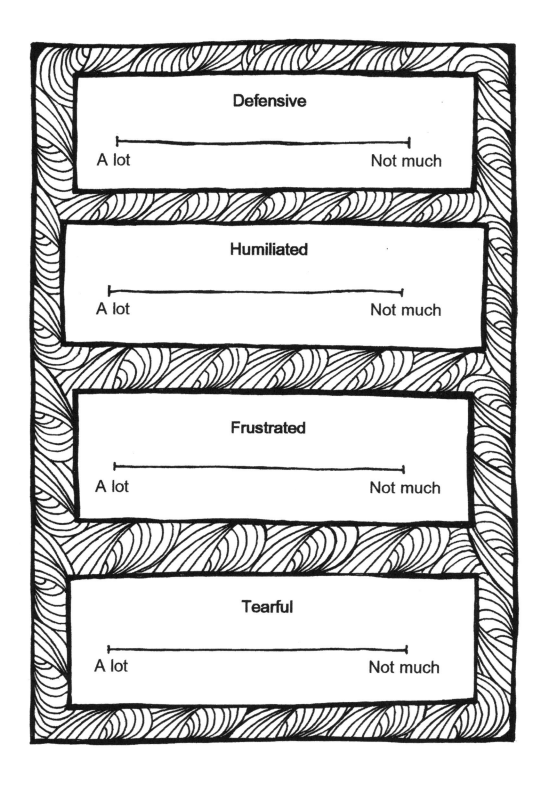

Defensive

A lot   Not much

Humiliated

A lot   Not much

Frustrated

A lot   Not much

Tearful

A lot   Not much

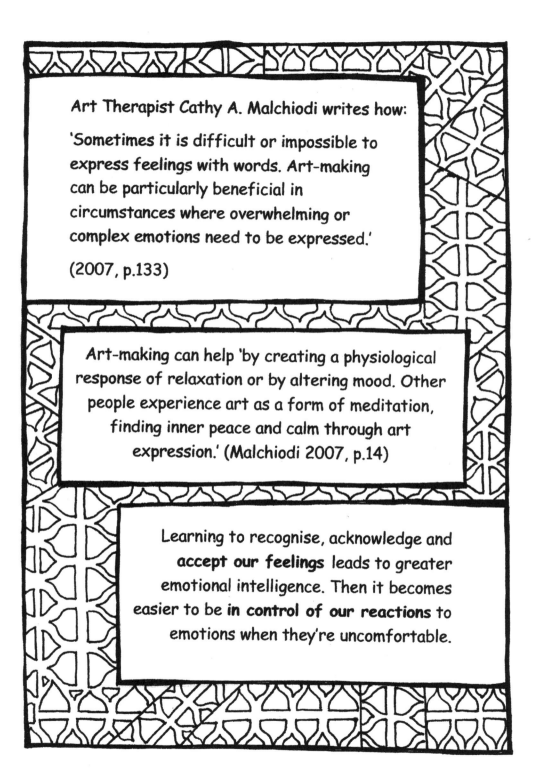

Art Therapist Cathy A. Malchiodi writes how:

'Sometimes it is difficult or impossible to express feelings with words. Art-making can be particularly beneficial in circumstances where overwhelming or complex emotions need to be expressed.'

(2007, p.133)

Art-making can help 'by creating a physiological response of relaxation or by altering mood. Other people experience art as a form of meditation, finding inner peace and calm through art expression.' (Malchiodi 2007, p.14)

Learning to recognise, acknowledge and **accept our feelings** leads to greater emotional intelligence. Then it becomes easier to be **in control of our reactions** to emotions when they're uncomfortable.

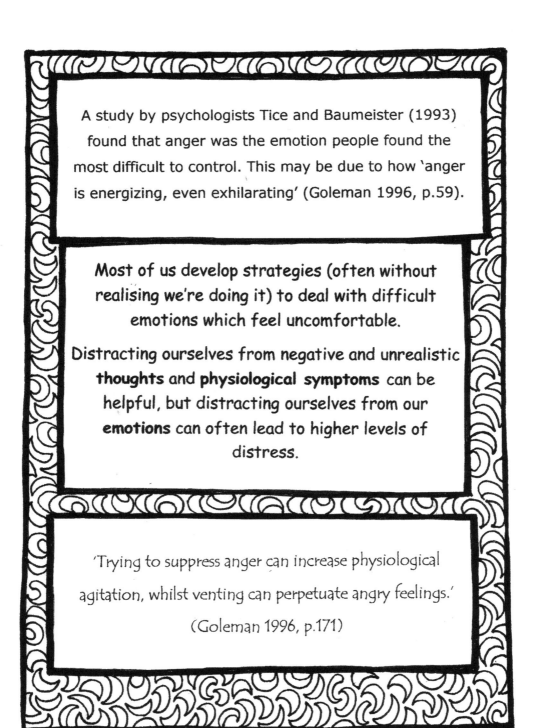

A study by psychologists Tice and Baumeister (1993) found that anger was the emotion people found the most difficult to control. This may be due to how 'anger is energizing, even exhilarating' (Goleman 1996, p.59).

Most of us develop strategies (often without realising we're doing it) to deal with difficult emotions which feel uncomfortable.

Distracting ourselves from negative and unrealistic **thoughts** and **physiological symptoms** can be helpful, but distracting ourselves from our **emotions** can often lead to higher levels of distress.

'Trying to suppress anger can increase physiological agitation, whilst venting can perpetuate angry feelings.' (Goleman 1996, p.171)

Beliefs about emotions

You can only start to **take control** of your emotions if you **believe that you can**, and this is essential for lowering emotional distress

(Winch 2018).

Draw a symbol on the scale to show whether you believe your emotions are fixed or malleable:

Fixed   Malleable

'Beliefs that individuals hold about whether emotions are malleable or fixed may play a crucial role in individuals' emotional experiences and their engagement in changing their emotions.'

(Kneeland *et al.* 2016, pp.81–88)

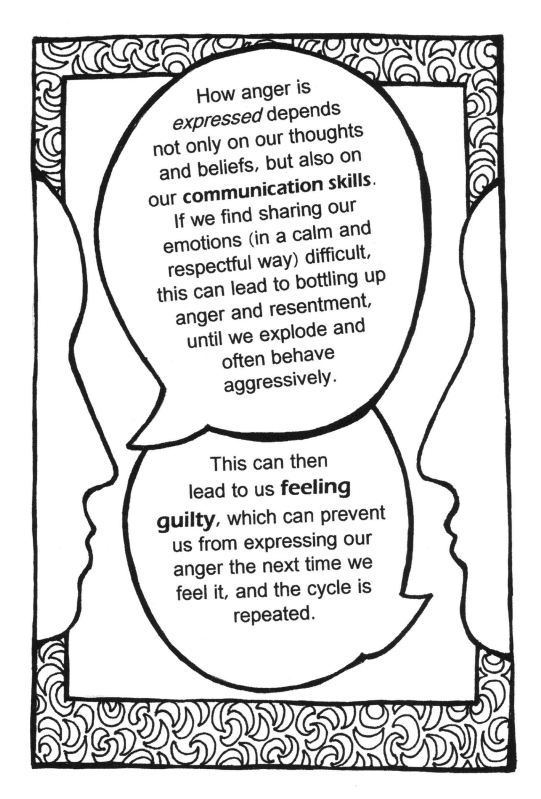

How anger is *expressed* depends not only on our thoughts and beliefs, but also on our **communication skills**. If we find sharing our emotions (in a calm and respectful way) difficult, this can lead to bottling up anger and resentment, until we explode and often behave aggressively.

This can then lead to us **feeling guilty**, which can prevent us from expressing our anger the next time we feel it, and the cycle is repeated.

If we try and increase
our confidence in expressing
emotions, this can really help to
prevent anger becoming bottled up.
On the following page, draw or
describe as many ways as you can
think of to express your anger safely
and respectfully.

Examples are:

- *Talking things through with someone such as a friend or therapist*

- *Using creative means such as making artwork or writing lyrics or poetry*

Ways I could express anger **safely** and **respectfully**.

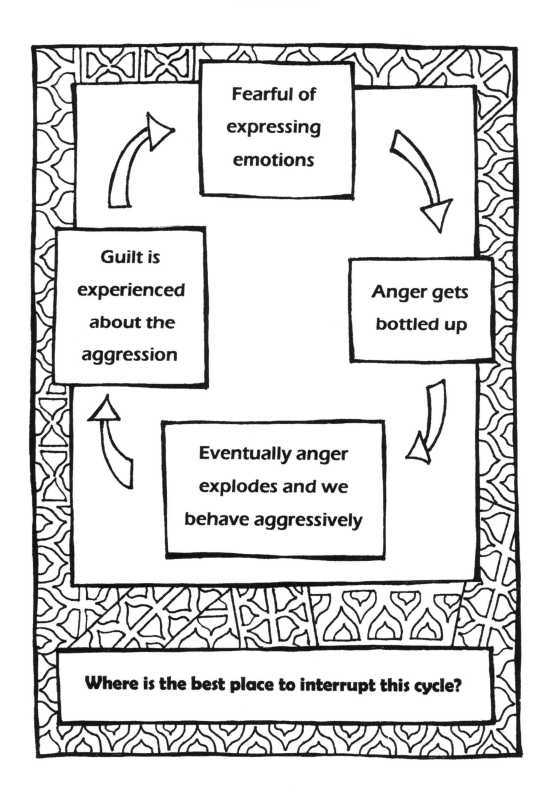

Fearful of expressing emotions

Anger gets bottled up

Eventually anger explodes and we behave aggressively

Guilt is experienced about the aggression

Where is the best place to interrupt this cycle?

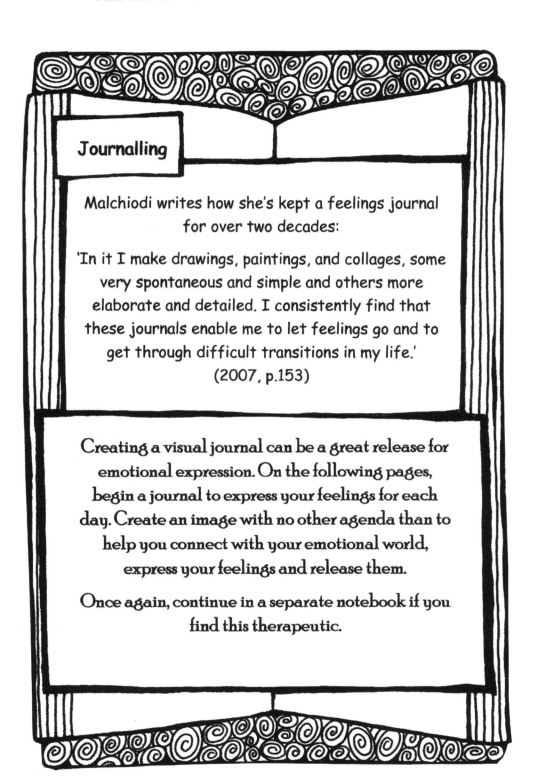

Journalling

Malchiodi writes how she's kept a feelings journal for over two decades:

'In it I make drawings, paintings, and collages, some very spontaneous and simple and others more elaborate and detailed. I consistently find that these journals enable me to let feelings go and to get through difficult transitions in my life.'
(2007, p.153)

Creating a visual journal can be a great release for emotional expression. On the following pages, begin a journal to express your feelings for each day. Create an image with no other agenda than to help you connect with your emotional world, express your feelings and release them.

Once again, continue in a separate notebook if you find this therapeutic.

Monday: I feel...

Wednesday: *I feel...*

Friday: *I feel...*

Saturday: *I feel...*

6

Behaviour

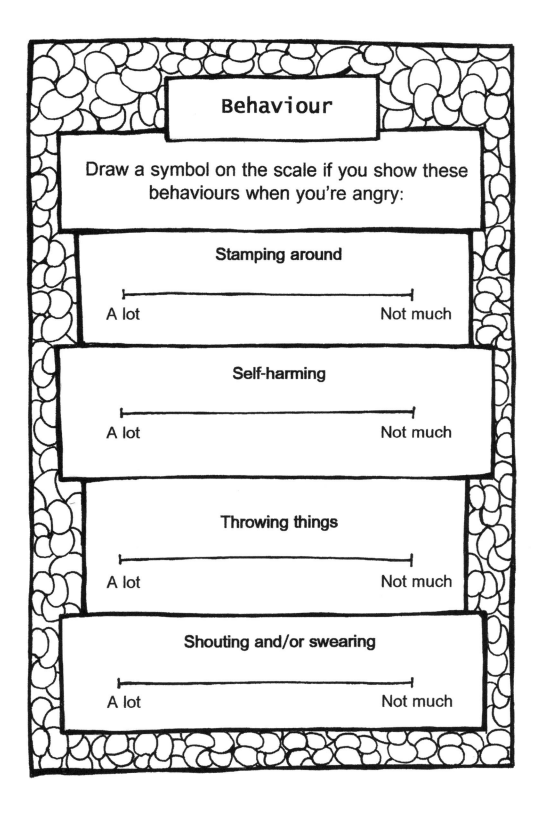

Behaviour

Draw a symbol on the scale if you show these behaviours when you're angry:

Stamping around

A lot ⊢————————————————⊣ Not much

Self-harming

A lot ⊢————————————————⊣ Not much

Throwing things

A lot ⊢————————————————⊣ Not much

Shouting and/or swearing

A lot ⊢————————————————⊣ Not much

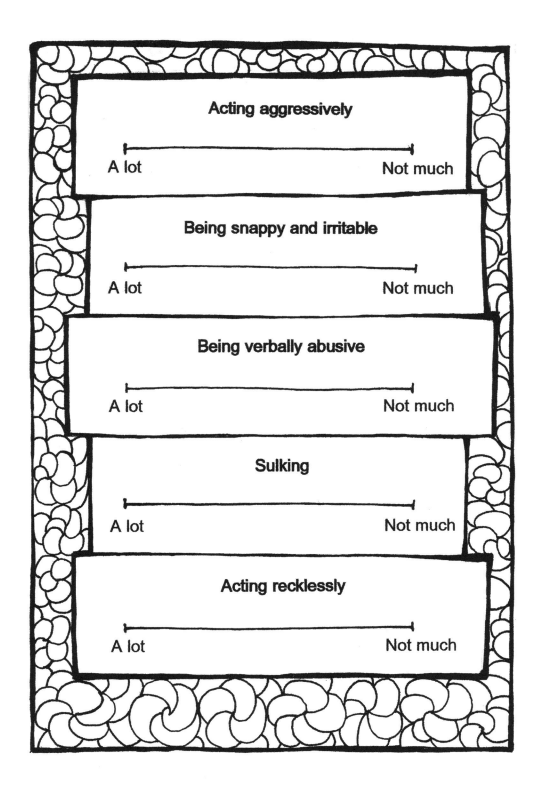

Acting aggressively

A lot   Not much

Being snappy and irritable

A lot   Not much

Being verbally abusive

A lot   Not much

Sulking

A lot   Not much

Acting recklessly

A lot   Not much

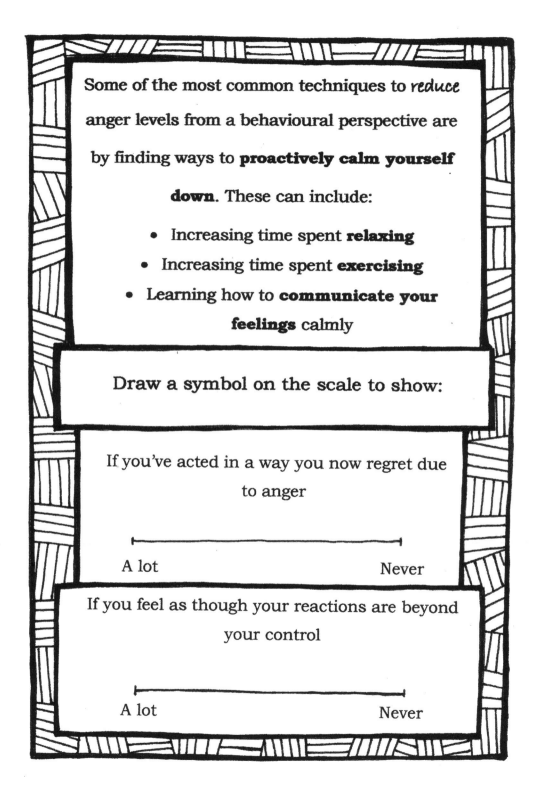

Some of the most common techniques to *reduce* anger levels from a behavioural perspective are by finding ways to **proactively calm yourself down**. These can include:

- Increasing time spent **relaxing**
- Increasing time spent **exercising**
- Learning how to **communicate your feelings** calmly

Draw a symbol on the scale to show:

If you've acted in a way you now regret due to anger

A lot   Never

If you feel as though your reactions are beyond your control

A lot   Never

- Do you feel in control of your time?
- How is your time spent?
- Are the activities you're doing increasing feelings of tension, stress and low mood?

'The *types* of activity you are doing are very important. Are your days full of pleasurable activities like talking to your friends, reading and arranging fun things to do? Or are they full of activities such as making breakfast for the family, commuting, going to work, answering emails, cleaning, paying bills and sorting out the mess that other people seem to have left for you? If the latter is more typical, then you might see why your mood could be low and your stress levels high.'

(Myles and Shafran 2015, p.142 and p.148)

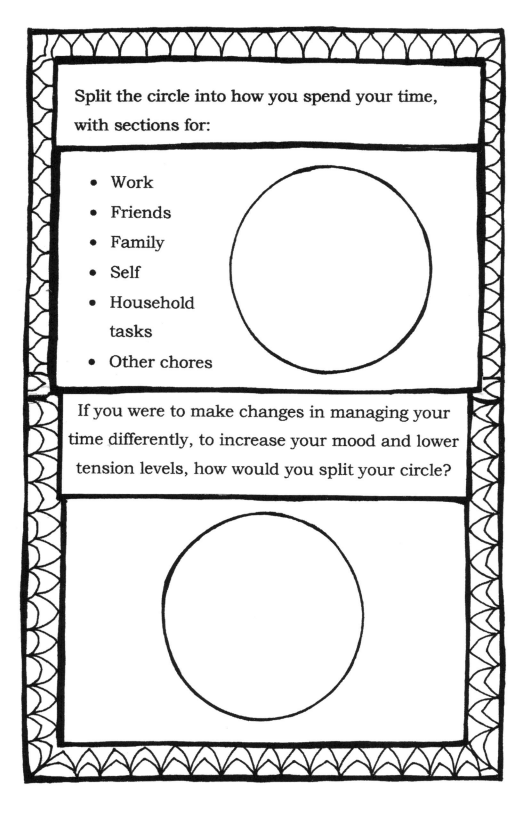

Split the circle into how you spend your time, with sections for:

- Work
- Friends
- Family
- Self
- Household tasks
- Other chores

If you were to make changes in managing your time differently, to increase your mood and lower tension levels, how would you split your circle?

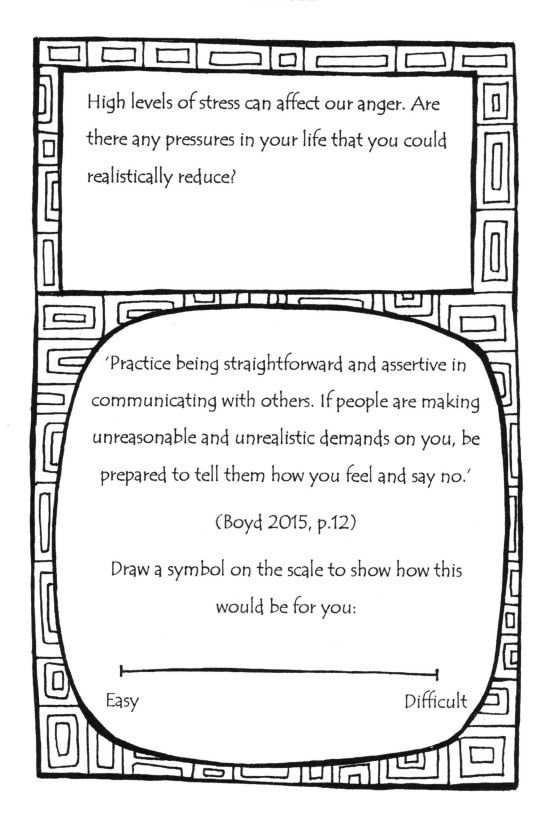

High levels of stress can affect our anger. Are there any pressures in your life that you could realistically reduce?

'Practice being straightforward and assertive in communicating with others. If people are making unreasonable and unrealistic demands on you, be prepared to tell them how you feel and say no.'

(Boyd 2015, p.12)

Draw a symbol on the scale to show how this would be for you:

Easy   Difficult

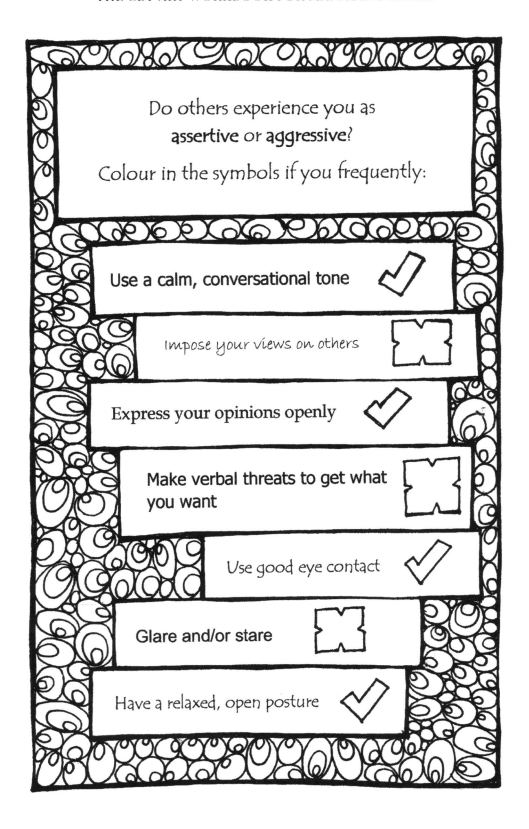

Do others experience you as **assertive** or **aggressive**?

Colour in the symbols if you frequently:

Use a calm, conversational tone ✓

Impose your views on others ✗

Express your opinions openly ✓

Make verbal threats to get what you want ✗

Use good eye contact ✓

Glare and/or stare ✗

Have a relaxed, open posture ✓

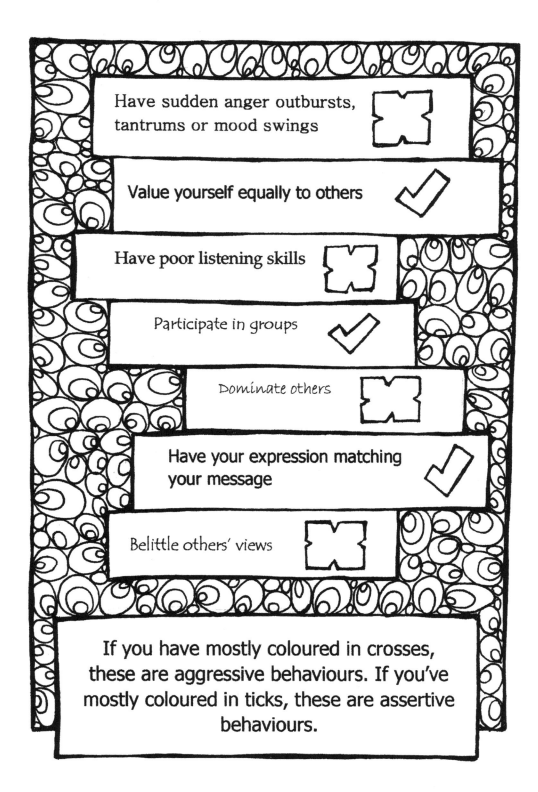

Have sudden anger outbursts, tantrums or mood swings ✖

Value yourself equally to others ✔

Have poor listening skills ✖

Participate in groups ✔

Dominate others ✖

Have your expression matching your message ✔

Belittle others' views ✖

If you have mostly coloured in crosses, these are aggressive behaviours. If you've mostly coloured in ticks, these are assertive behaviours.

If we were brought up without learning skills to deal with and effectively communicate our emotions, or where high levels of anger were expressed by those around us, there's a likelihood we will go on to develop anger problems (Myles and Shafran 2015).

If you'd like to be more respected than feared by those around you, you might need to express yourself in an assertive, rather than aggressive way.

To do this it may help to:

- Become more aware of and connect more with your own emotions
- Increase your awareness of others' emotions
- Be respectful of others' opinions and feelings
- Improve your listening skills

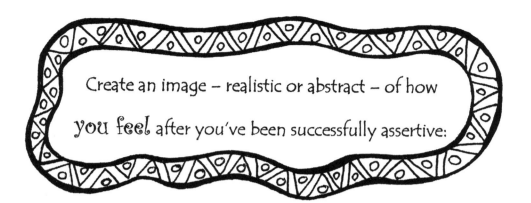

Create an image – realistic or abstract – of how you feel after you've been successfully assertive:

7

Physiology

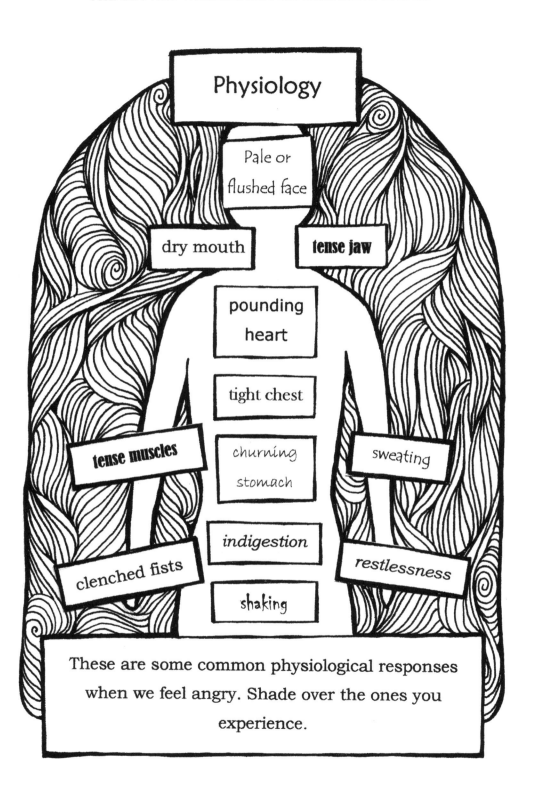

Physiology

Pale or flushed face

dry mouth

tense jaw

pounding heart

tight chest

tense muscles

churning stomach

sweating

indigestion

restlessness

clenched fists

shaking

These are some common physiological responses when we feel angry. Shade over the ones you experience.

Research has shown that frequently experiencing high levels of anger can have a serious impact on our physical health, such as increasing high blood pressure and lowering our immune system:

'People who experienced unremitting tension or hostility were found to have *double* the risk of heart disease – including asthma, arthritis, headaches, peptic ulcers, and heart disease.

Chronic anger need not be a death sentence: hostility is a habit that can change.'

(Goleman 1996, pp.169–171)

The brain

'The amygdala is held responsible for many of our emotions, including anger. When we get really angry it is sometimes referred to as an amygdala-hijack. The amygdala belongs to our "primitive brain". So, a primitive part of the brain hijacks the cerebral cortex…our thinking, planning, rational, executive-function part of the brain. The primitive brain always reacts much more quickly than the cerebral cortex.

When we "lose it" this is quite a major event inside our head. The control we normally have is through the thinking, executive-function part of the brain and it is this that we lose when the amygdala hijacks the whole process.'

(Davies 2016, pp.6–7)

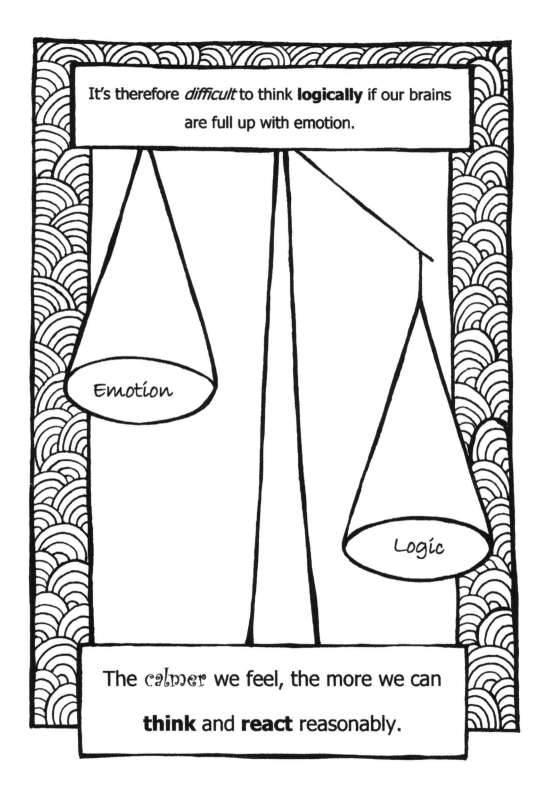

It's therefore *difficult* to think **logically** if our brains are full up with emotion.

Emotion

Logic

The calmer we feel, the more we can **think** and **react** reasonably.

'When the body is already in a state of edginess, and something triggers an emotional hijacking, the subsequent emotion, whether anger or anxiety, is of especially great intensity. Anger builds on anger; the emotional brain heats up.'

(Goleman 1996, p.60)

Physical symptoms can be a helpful tool in alerting us to our thoughts, and learning how to reduce these physiological responses can help **reduce anger levels**.

Some common ways are:

- Using guided imagery and meditation
- Practising focused breathing
- Being in nature
- Reducing consumption of stimulants
- Practising relaxation techniques
- Using focused distraction techniques
- Increasing exercise

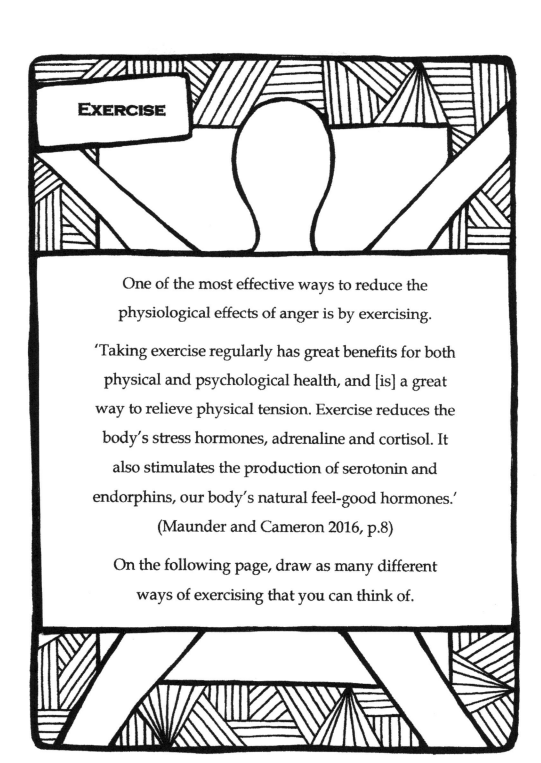

EXERCISE

One of the most effective ways to reduce the physiological effects of anger is by exercising.

'Taking exercise regularly has great benefits for both physical and psychological health, and [is] a great way to relieve physical tension. Exercise reduces the body's stress hormones, adrenaline and cortisol. It also stimulates the production of serotonin and endorphins, our body's natural feel-good hormones.' (Maunder and Cameron 2016, p.8)

On the following page, draw as many different ways of exercising that you can think of.

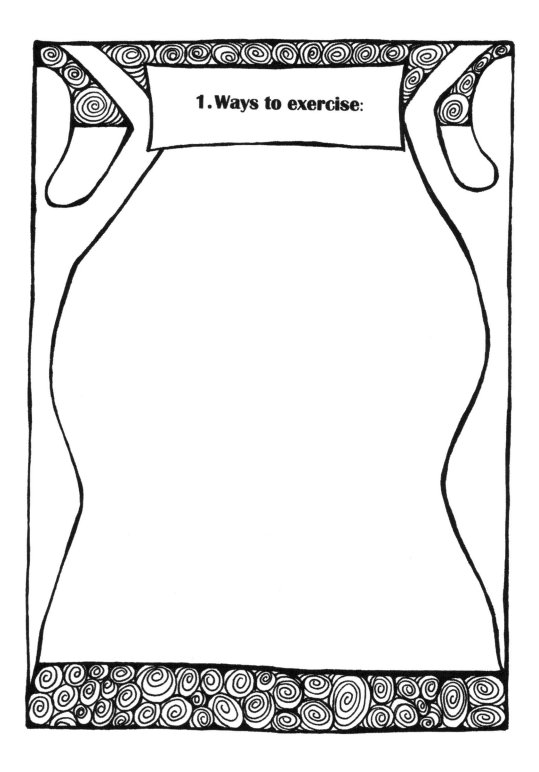

1. Ways to exercise:

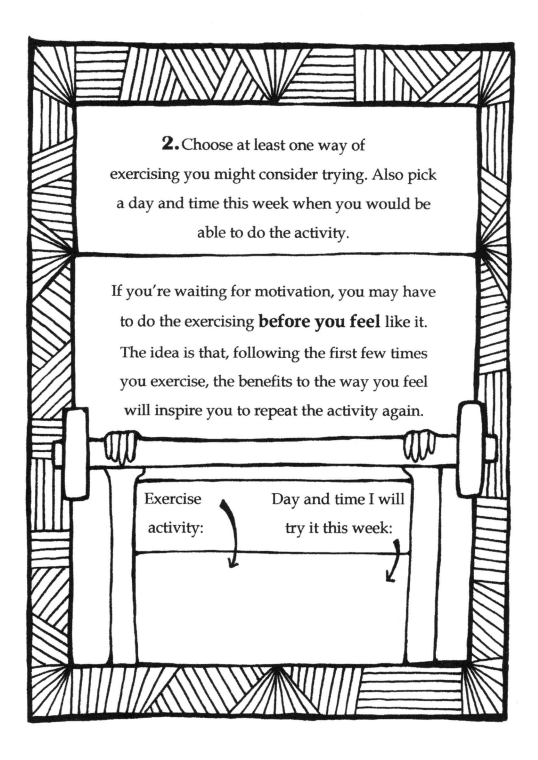

2. Choose at least one way of exercising you might consider trying. Also pick a day and time this week when you would be able to do the activity.

If you're waiting for motivation, you may have to do the exercising **before you feel** like it. The idea is that, following the first few times you exercise, the benefits to the way you feel will inspire you to repeat the activity again.

Exercise activity:

Day and time I will try it this week:

If you **imagine, perceive** or **experience** being under threat or in danger, your body will respond. Adrenaline and cortisol will be released into your system in preparation for dealing with the danger (Maunder and Cameron 2016).

Whether the danger is perceived or imagined doesn't matter to our **physiological responses**. Likewise, if you imagine a place of safety where you feel **relaxed** and **calm,** your body will respond to this also.

The more you focus on the **sensory aspects** of being in this place of safety, the more powerful your physiological reaction will be.

On the following two pages, complete the images to include:

- What you can see, hear, smell and touch
- Are you alone or with others?
- What is the weather like?

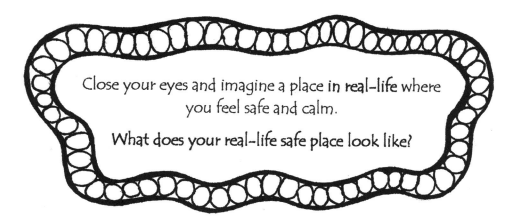

Close your eyes and imagine a place in real-life where you feel safe and calm.

What does your real-life safe place look like?

Close your eyes and picture an **imaginary place** where you feel safe and calm.

What does your imaginary safe place look like?

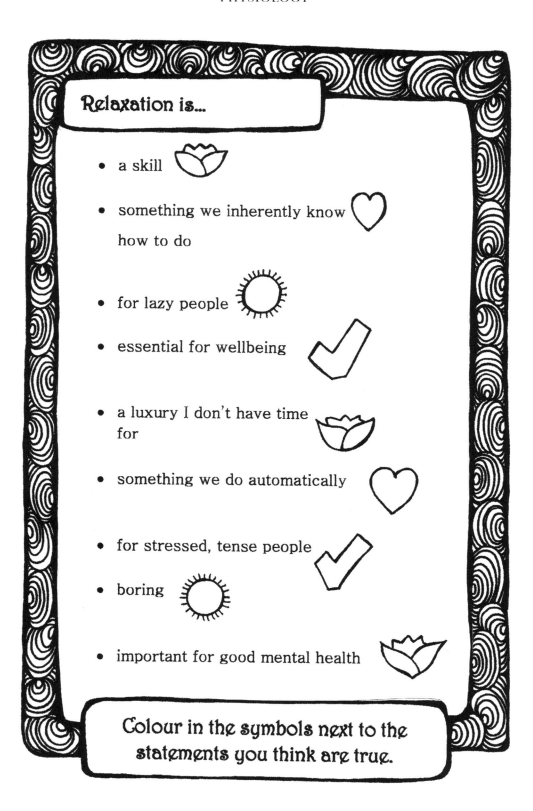

Relaxation is...

- a skill
- something we inherently know how to do
- for lazy people
- essential for wellbeing
- a luxury I don't have time for
- something we do automatically
- for stressed, tense people
- boring
- important for good mental health

Colour in the symbols next to the statements you think are true.

Draw or describe the last time you felt relaxed:

Only you can carve out some time in your daily life to devote to relaxation. It's more likely to happen if you decide now how regularly you'd like to give your time for doing this.

'Learning how to relax can be particularly helpful if you are experiencing anger problems.'

(Goleman 1996, p.210)

We may know this and realise it's a good idea, yet we only feel the benefits when we **practise** relaxation techniques regularly.

Most of us have learned what helps us relax, and some different ways we can do this effectively. It's helpful for many physiological symptoms, such as:

- Lowering blood pressure
- Slowing breathing rate
- Reducing tension in muscles
- Calming brain activity
- Improving concentration
- Reducing the release of stress hormones

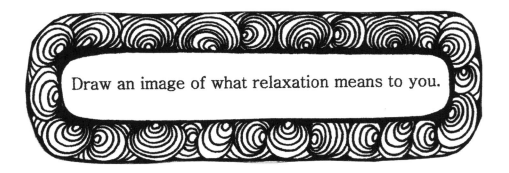

Draw an image of what relaxation means to you.

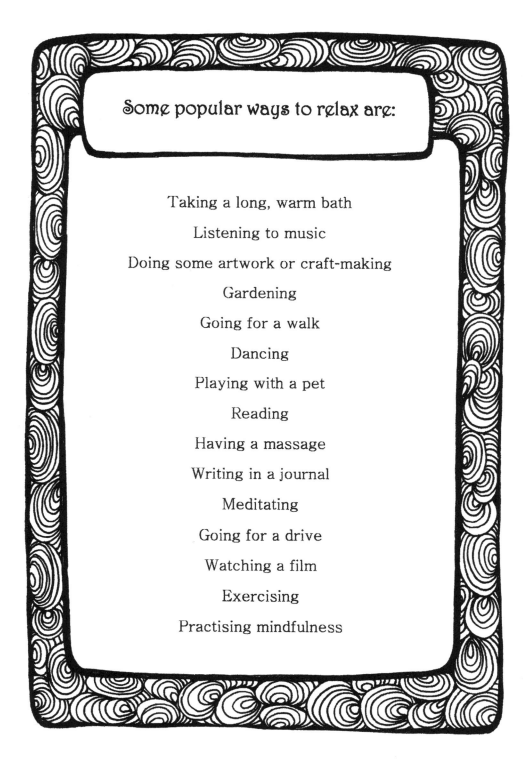

Some popular ways to relax are:

Taking a long, warm bath

Listening to music

Doing some artwork or craft-making

Gardening

Going for a walk

Dancing

Playing with a pet

Reading

Having a massage

Writing in a journal

Meditating

Going for a drive

Watching a film

Exercising

Practising mindfulness

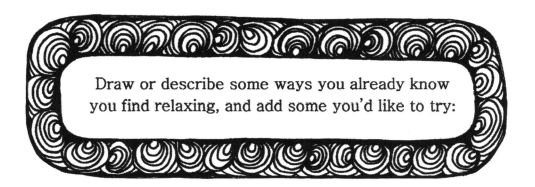

Draw or describe some ways you already know you find relaxing, and add some you'd like to try:

In the next week...

On how many days, for how much time, is it possible for you to include some relaxation time?

Draw a symbol to represent the relaxing activity you could do on which day/time:

Day	Time	Relaxation exercise
Monday		
Tuesday		
Wednesday		
Thursday		
Friday		
Saturday		
Sunday		

8

Staying Calm

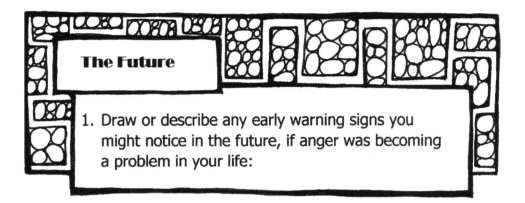

The Future

1. Draw or describe any early warning signs you might notice in the future, if anger was becoming a problem in your life:

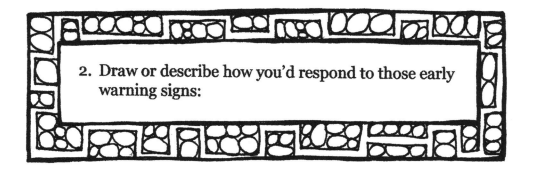

2. Draw or describe how you'd respond to those early warning signs:

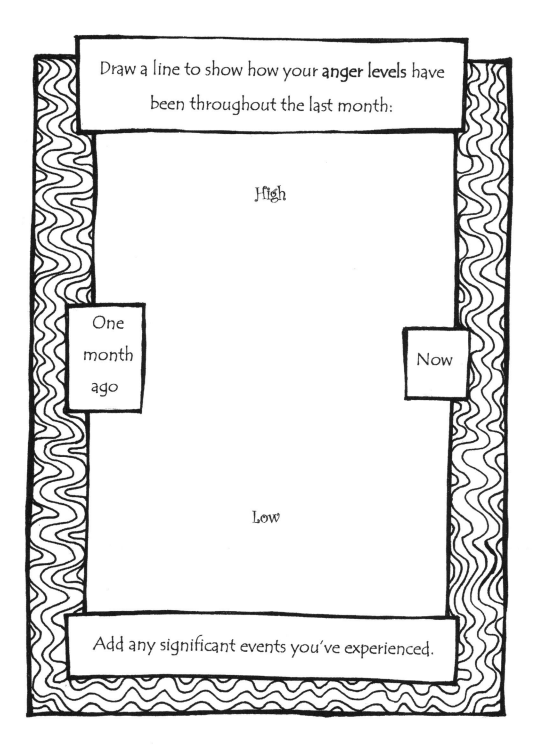

Draw a line to show how your **anger levels** have been throughout the last month:

High

One month ago

Now

Low

Add any significant events you've experienced.

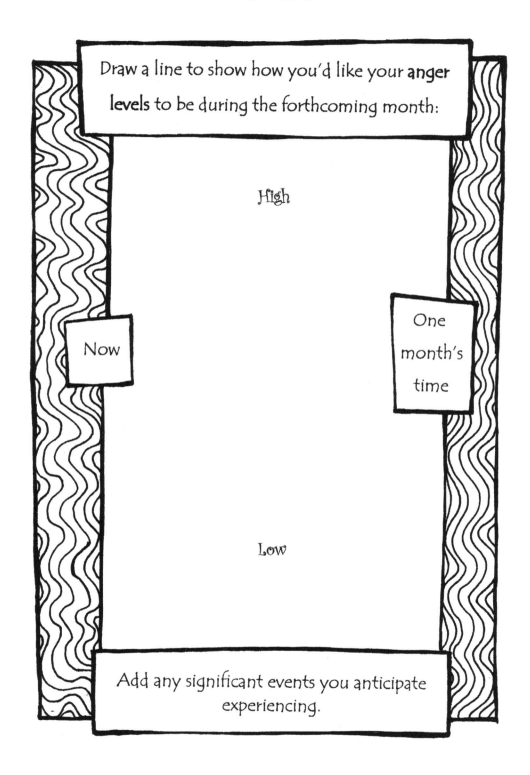

Draw a line to show how you'd like your **anger** levels to be during the forthcoming month:

High

Now

One month's time

Low

Add any significant events you anticipate experiencing.

If you were to create an image – realistic or abstract – to show what **serenity** means to you, what would this look like?

If you were to create an image – realistic or abstract – to show what *peace* means to you, what would this look like?

If you were to create an image – realistic or abstract – to show what **joy** means to you, what would this look like?

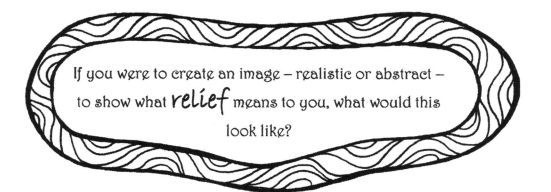

If you were to create an image – realistic or abstract – to show what **relief** means to you, what would this look like?

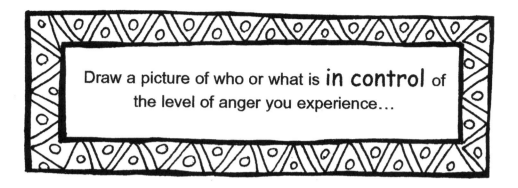

Draw a picture of who or what is **in control** of the level of anger you experience…

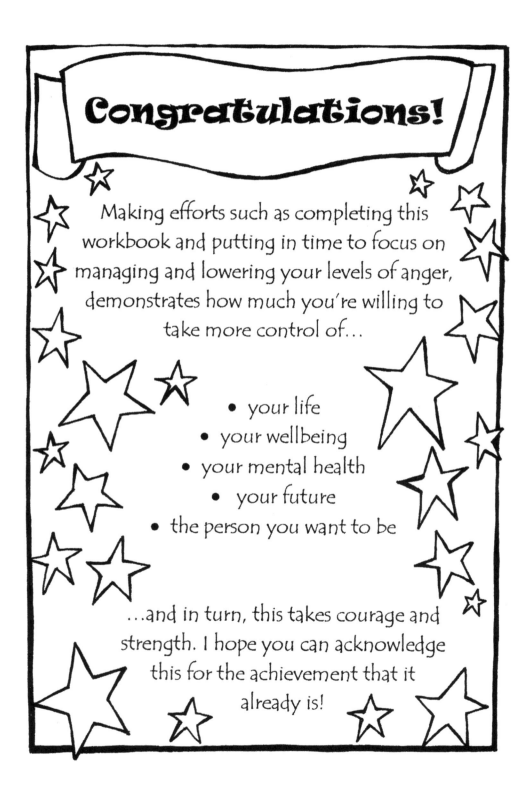

Congratulations!

Making efforts such as completing this workbook and putting in time to focus on managing and lowering your levels of anger, demonstrates how much you're willing to take more control of…

- your life
- your wellbeing
- your mental health
- your future
- the person you want to be

…and in turn, this takes courage and strength. I hope you can acknowledge this for the achievement that it already is!

References

Barford, D. (2018) 'Dark night of the soul.' *Therapy Today*, Vol 29(6): 35.

Beck, J.S. (1995) *Cognitive Therapy: Basics and Beyond*. New York, NY: Guilford Press.

Boyd, R. (2015) *How to Manage Stress*. Available at: www.mind.org.uk/media/1993364/how-to-manage-stress_2015.pdf.

Davies, W. (2016) *Overcoming Anger and Irritability*. London: Robinson.

Goleman, D. (1996) *Emotional Intelligence*. London: Bloomsbury.

Kneeland, E.T., Dovidio, J.F., Joormann, J. and Clark, M.S. (2016) 'Emotion malleability beliefs, emotion regulation, and psychopathology: Integrating affective and clinical science.' *Clinical Psychology Review*, April 45:81–88. Available at: www.ncbi.nlm.nih.gov/pubmed/27086086.

London, P. (1989) *No More Secondhand Art: Awakening the Artist Within*. Boston, MA: Shambala.

Malchiodi, C.A. (2007) *The Art Therapy Sourcebook*. New York, NY: McGraw Hill.

Manning, J. and Ridgeway, N. (2016) *CBT Worksheets for Anxiety*. Bury St Edmunds, Suffolk: West Suffolk CBT Service Ltd.

Maunder, L., Cameron, L. and Charlton, F. (2016) *Controlling Anger*. Newcastle: Northumberland, Tyne and Wear NHS Foundation Trust.

Maunder, L. and Cameron, L. (2016) *Anxiety and Panic*. Newcastle: Northumberland, Tyne and Wear NHS Foundation Trust.

Myles, P. and Shafran, R. (2015) *The CBT Handbook*. London: Robinson.

Neenan, M. and Dryden, W. (2004) *Cognitive Therapy: 100 Key Points and Techniques*. Hove: Brunner Routledge.

Tice, D. and Baumeister, R. (1993) 'Controlling anger: Self-induced emotion change.' In D. Wegner and J. Pennebaker (eds.) *The Handbook of Mental Control*. New Jersey: Prentice-Hall, Inc.

Winch, G. (2018) 'Why you should believe you can control your emotions.' *Psychology Today*. Available at: www.psychologytoday.com/gb/blog/the-squeaky-wheel/201809/why-you-should-believe-you-can-control-your-emotions (posted 5 Sep 18).